Drugs, Sex and Dirty Politics

Drugs, Sex and Dirty Politics

*One man's battle for Legalization
against a corrupt system*

BY DALTON DANIELS

Charleston, SC
www.PalmettoPublishing.com

Sex, Drugs, and Dirty Politics
Copyright © 2023 by Dalton Daniels

First Edition

Hardcover: 979-8-8229-0260-2
Paperback: 979-8-8229-0261-9
eBook: 979-8-8229-0262-6

D

I want to dedicate this book to Jack Herrer (author of *The Emperor Wears No Clothes*) for being an outspoken proponent of legalization and opponent of government corruption. This is also dedicated to the thousands of people who have lost their lives and their freedom because of a simple plant. Sorry, Jack…I don't think any apologies are coming anytime soon. Rest in peace.

Contents

The Truth about the Plant ix

Chapter 1: Smoking Funny Things 1

Chapter 2: When Opportunity Knocks. 6

Chapter 3: On The Ground in Los Angeles 20

Chapter 4: Decision Time. 47

Chapter 5: Moving Forward 52

Chapter 6: The Move to Los Angeles 84

Chapter 7: Grand Opening. 96

Chapter 8: The Big Bang. 116

Chapter 9: Trouble on Two Fronts 124

Chapter 10: The LA City Council. 132

Chapter 11: The Eyes of a Nation 150

Chapter 12: Hardship Review. 158

Chapter 13: Council Bluffs 178

Chapter 14: Feliz Navidad. 181

Chapter 15: Petition Fails 190

Chapter 16: A New Direction. 195

Chapter 17: Battle Stations 206

Chapter 18: Pulling the Tail of the Tiger 213

Chapter 19: Rise of Kamala Harris 223

Chapter 20: Escape from LA 227

The Truth about the Plant

T he truth of the matter is…no one wants to know the truth. We are all content to believe that our police, our politicians, and our government are here to protect us and serve us. Whom are they really protecting? Whom do they really serve? Since before man walked on the earth, the plant grew freely from the ground as God or nature intended. Occasionally an animal might come along to eat the leaves of the plant. The once cautious and alert animal would then become relaxed and worry-free, only to be devoured by a predator. Is it better to live in fear every day of your life or better to die relaxed and free from fear?

As man came on the scene, he grew fond of the plant. Over many centuries, they lived together in peace and harmony with nature. Until, as history repeats, they were attacked and annihilated by a predator. Usually, this predator was another race of men. An angry race. One driven by greed and power. A race not calmed by the plant.

The leaders of men then decided: Is it not better to keep men fearful? Fear creates action. Action creates productivity. Productivity creates wealth. Wealth creates power. For this reason, fear is certainly better than tranquility. The leaders then took the plant away. Tensions grew. Productivity increased. Wars were fought. Power and wealth were established. All at the cost of lives that the leaders determined to be collateral damage.

A small few remained in the shadows. They stayed with the plant and avoided these calamities that had befallen mankind, but the police sought these men out and imprisoned them. Their money and their homes were taken. Their families were shattered. Their lives were destroyed. All for seeking the peace of the plant.

"How dare men seek tranquility in such a violent world?" the leaders said.

But the leaders knew the truth. If you control the plant, you control the wealth and power of the world. The plant was a gift from the gods exploited by man for his own evil purposes. The war on the plant is a war on mankind.

Chapter 1: Smoking Funny Things
1982

I f you have ever tried smoking a joint, then you know the very first time you probably didn't inhale.

Much has been made of Bill Clinton's famous comment about his first time smoking weed. The funny part is, for most of us who have smoked pot, we know the comment was probably a true statement.

Most likely, for your first time, you were out with a group of friends and were not expecting marijuana to be introduced into the situation.

I was sixteen years old and a junior in high school. I had been invited to a party by one of the cheerleaders, Dana, of our football team, and everyone who was anyone was going. It seems her parents were going out of town and trusting her and her sister to act responsibly. They obviously didn't know their daughters very well.

Her house was located on the north shore of Eagle Lake, which was a medium-sized lake just outside of town. I went to the party with my good friend Iggy; I had been hanging out with him a lot lately. He and I had just made the varsity football team, and both of us played the inside linebacker positions as co-captains. When we arrived, the party was already rocking, with about thirty people in attendance. As we walked through the house, there were a few of the other cheerleaders, Nancy and Jody, hanging out with Dana in the kitchen. I had always had a little crush on Nancy. They were doing shots of peppermint schnapps on the center island and offered one to Iggy and me as we walked through. Not wanting to seem nerdy, we accepted, and both Iggy and I tossed one back. It was strong and harsh and took me by surprise. It reminded me of drinking mouthwash. I looked at Iggy, and he looked at me. Then he howled, "Party!" as only Iggy could do, in his usual *Animal House* manner. To be honest, this was only the second time I had tried alcohol. The first time, I had stolen a beer out of my dad's fridge and taken a swig…only to spit it out in the sink.

"How could anyone drink that crap?" I wondered naively.

The sliding glass doors were opened in the kitchen, which led to the backyard and the boat dock. Outside, I saw a few more members of our team, so I told Iggy to follow me as we walked to the back. As I walked out back, I heard a familiar "Danyo" from a familiar voice.

It was Dale, another member of my team, and he was hanging out with Bunky and "Taco," two more teammates. Dale motioned us over, and as we approached; I saw a spiral of smoke exit his nostrils. In his hand he was holding a white "cigarette," but the smell coming off it was definitely not tobacco. I looked at Bunky and Taco and could tell their eyes were glazed over, and they both had stupid grins on their faces.

"Are you ready to take a slow ride?" Dale said in a playfully stoned manner. He proceeded to pretend to be playing air guitar to the song blasting from the boom box. The band was Fog Hat, I believe.

Now, drinking was one thing, but I swore I would never try drugs. I looked at Iggy; he looked at me. "I don't know. Iggy, what do you think?"

"Don't be a puss," Dale chided Iggy.

"Fuck you," Iggy said as he grabbed the joint and took a toke.

Then he handed it to me. To keep my newly found "cool" status, I did the same and then handed the joint back to Dale. At that point, I made an excuse to move away from the group, Iggy in tow, and we found some other kids hanging by the pier. The party continued for a few more hours until the cops arrived, and we all filtered out quickly.

That first time, I didn't inhale. In fact, the first couple of times I didn't inhale. Then, when I finally did inhale, I didn't get high. Or if I did, I just felt a little silly or sleepy. Not the Dangerous narcotic that your parents warned you about. I remember when I finally started feeling "high," I would just laugh about nothing and forget all my worries for a while. I also started to forget a lot of things…and lose a lot of things. My school work started to suffer and relationships, which were already bizarre at age sixteen, became even more confusing and complex.

I grew up in a small town in Michigan called Edwardsburg, with a population of a thousand, give or take a few. We had only one stop light and no McDonalds. Life was rough…we had to cook our own hamburgers. There were more bars in town than churches, and everyone knew everyone. It was primarily a white working-class town. The area was dotted with small lakes and surrounded by cornfields on all sides. On a Friday or Saturday night, it was common for my high school friends and me to go find a place in the woods or fields or to go to the Lake Michigan dunes together to drink a few beers, "sipping whiskey out the bottle, not thinking 'bout tomorrow," and, yes, to smoke a couple of doobies.

Summers were short and humid, with tons of mosquitoes and gnats to spoil any party. Winters were cold and harsh, with snowstorms that could bury your whole house and cut you off from the outside world.

As you can imagine, the youth of the town would get bored and restless with no PlayStation or internet to engulf our minds, so drinking and smoking pot seemed like a good way to cut through the boredom. The awkwardness of youth toward the opposite sex kind of diminishes after a good buzz sets in, so once you find a little country girl who likes to take a puff, the natural progression leads to clothes coming off and windows becoming foggy.

It all seemed pretty harmless…unlike the opioid addictions of today.

One night, in my senior year, three of my football buddies and I were out blowing a doob and drinking a few beers on a gravel road when, all of a sudden, red and blue lights came up behind us.

"Oh crap," my buddy Rob, the quarterback of our team, said. "Eat the joint, Dalton. Just eat it."

Now, I was still a little leery of the possible effects of marijuana on my stomach. All I could do was imagine getting my stomach pumped. Instead, I extinguished the joint, and we all rolled down the windows. I'm sure the officer got quite the chuckle out of the fact that smoke came billowing out the windows like a scene from a Cheech and Chong movie. I hid the roach under the seat as the officer approached.

The Edwardsburg police department, in all its glory, consisted of four cops and two squad cars. None of them could be considered of above-average intelligence, but this one had us dead to rights. He asked us to step out of the car and began rummaging through the vehicle. One by one, he placed the open cans of beer, the empty cans, and what was left of the twelve-pack on the gravel road.

"You boys been smoking marijuana?" he asked.

"No, sir," we denied vehemently.

He continued to search the car until he discovered it under my seat.

"Then what is this?" he asked, like the cat who had just caught the canary.

We were all loaded into his car and taken down to the station. We all sat in dead silence, imagining our fates when our parents found out.

The Edwardsburg police station, at the time, was not much more than a trailer with a reception area and a couple of offices. Not too many hardened criminals were ever found there, and I'm not sure they even had a holding cell. We were asked to sit in the waiting room and one by one were called back to speak to the officer.

"Now, you boys aren't under arrest," he said. "I'm just gonna let your parents know, and they can decide your punishment."

"What's the name and phone number of your father?" he asked me.

After all the parents had been called, we all walked out into the waiting room again, awaiting our fates.

Randy, the biggest boy, who played nose tackle on our team, seemed the most distraught.

"My dad's gonna beat the crap out of me," he sobbed. He repeated this many times.

I really didn't know what my stepdad would do or say. We were never really close, and he had never struck me when I was younger. Now that I was much bigger and could bench 300 lb., I didn't think it was a good time to start.

The first parent to arrive was Mr. Borden, Rob's dad. He was also my social studies teacher, and I must admit that I was a little embarrassed when our eyes met. He had always bragged about what a good student I was.

"Let's go," he said to Rob. With that, Rob walked out into the darkness.

My dad arrived next. Without a word, I stood up and made my way to the door. My last memory was seeing poor Randy hunched over, head in hands, half sobbing about his upcoming doom.

Chapter 2: When Opportunity Knocks
Twenty Six Years Later; November 2008

It was a Tuesday night and I was sitting in front of the television, debating whether I should go out to the casinos for some Texas Hold'em. I'd been blowing a lot of money lately just trying to avoid death by boredom.

You see, it was late November of 2008. Barack Obama had just won the presidency but had not taken office yet. I had just returned from a three-week trip to Ukraine, searching for love on one of those "find a Russian bride" trips advertised online. It had been my second trip to Odessa, where I had decided to end my long-term relationship with a young lady named Marina, whom I had been dating for the last two years. While dating hot Russian women probably rates high on every man's Richter scale, you'll have to read my next book to hear about my exploits over there. I had finally come to the conclusion that dating Ukrainian/Russian women was like dating a Klingon female. Everything was way too damn serious, with little emotion or affection. They had absolutely no clue how to have fun and looked at Americans as "big children," or so I was told. This trip in particular had gotten a little dangerous at the end, so I had decided to return to the US early. Dating Russian women was just another way to stop the perpetual boredom. Life was just dragging by.

You see, back in 2006, for my fortieth birthday, I had decided to sell everything and explore the world. I had been working a job, or sometimes two, since the age of fourteen and thought it was time to take some time for myself. I wanted to answer for myself the question, "If money was no object and you could do whatever you wanted, what would you do? Who would you be? Who would you hang out with? Is there something else out there besides the day-to-day grind of owning a business or working a job?"

So I sold my business of ten years, and I sold my party house at the top of the real estate bubble and walked away with about a half million dollars cash. Now, my family advised me to do the right thing and invest the money. Play it safe and wait for old age to kill me, right? Or perhaps settle down with a good woman. Maybe start a second family? No, thanks. Been there, done that, got the T-shirt.

I decided to do the irresponsible thing...and set out to see the world. Live life on the edge and just enjoy every day as it comes. I made several trips to Europe and spent New Year's Eve of 2006 in Amsterdam. I then started dating Russian beauties from 2006 to 2008. I thoroughly enjoyed the freedoms that fortune had provided—no schedules and no one to answer to. My kids were grown. Life was good. But eventually, boredom crept back into the picture, which no amount of partying and drinking could take away.

When I finally decided it was time to get back to the real world, I realized I was down to my last $200,000. Now again, I must stress, remember what the economy was like in late 2008. The housing bubble had burst, and the stock market had crashed. Most people I knew had lost everything. Cash was *king*, and I had it. Because $200,000 was like a million at that time, I wasn't worried. I also had incredible credit with several hundred thousand dollars available on credit lines. I had no debt and no dependents. I guess being lazy and irresponsible had paid off. But there was still one big problem. Since all the markets were still in free fall, even though I had cash and credit...Where was the opportunity? All of my business savvy and all my contacts were useless unless I could find a growing market. I looked at franchises, bars, restaurants, and even a white-water rafting company, but no business was doing well. I wanted to do something interesting…something exciting…something outside the box. But the average Joe did not have expendable income, so most businesses were struggling to stay alive or failing with no money and no customers.

This is why I spent my days trying to perfect my skills as a Texas Hold'em player. After all, I believed I was smarter than the average bear, and this didn't look that complicated. This was about the same time that the world poker tournament started to be televised. After a year, I realized I was no Phil Ivey.

So here I was on the couch, on a Tuesday night, the most boring night of the week, watching Fox News. The election was a month past, and Barack was offering hope and change.

At about 8:00 p.m., the phone rang. It was an old business associate named Brian Kim. Now, I didn't know Brian all that well, but I had met him several years earlier at my place of business. You see, I had started a company back in 1999 called Adventures 2000. It was basically a service that provided over thirty events per month for single professionals in the Phoenix area.

I had started the company on a shoestring budget by borrowing $2,000 from a friend, and in the course of five years, I had built it into a million-dollar-per-year enterprise. I guess I fall into the 2 percent of natural-born entrepreneurs. I had met Brian one day when he had basically cold-called my business, trying to capture some of my $25,000 monthly advertising budget. His advertising scheme didn't work out so well, but he seemed like a sharp business guy, so we kept in touch.

Brian Kim was a small, well-fed American of Korean descent. I, being somewhat of a Michigan country boy, had never really spent much time around people of different ethnicities, which created a huge curiosity for me. In fact, that could probably explain my search for love in foreign countries.

So, Brian was on the phone that night and asked if we could get together. Now, hanging out with a Korean businessman is about as fun as watching plastic grass grow…but again, I was looking for an opportunity, so I wanted to pick his brain. Brian always had his hands in something. In fact, Brian had made a small fortune in the real estate bubble in Phoenix.

The market had been rising so fast in Arizona that Brian had perfected a way to put a $5,000 deposit on a new build house. This deposit would then secure the contract for the house. Because there was such a backlog of houses to be built, the house would not be completed for eighteen months. During that same period, the value of the finished house would appreciate by $50,000, and Brian would just sell the contract for $50,000 and pocket the $45,000 profit. He had done this over fifty times, netting over two million dollars. Not a bad little scheme and 100 percent legal. So when Brian calls, Dalton listens.

We agreed to meet at my favorite little sports bar on the Greenbelt in Scottsdale named Dukes. After having a few drinks, we decided to go back to my place and have a few more beers. Upon leaving, Brian tipped his usual $1 tip. Why is it that rich people always seem to be the cheapest when it comes to tips? I guess I will never be rich then. I threw an extra $5 on the pot, to cover the both of us.

Once back to my house, Brian just sat and started at the TV, not really saying anything. I would try to break the silence occasionally, but Brian would just answer with a short, non-expansive answer. When I was about to call it a night, Brian finally began a conversation. Looking back now, this is what he had been thinking about the whole time and just was not sure how to present it.

"Have you ever heard of Medical marijuana" He asked, very directly and with a nervous laugh?

"Not really", I replied. "What is that?"

"Oh..in California, marijuana is legal, for medical patients"

"Oh my god…are you serious?" I asked in disbelief. "Leave it to those damn Californians to figure out a way to smoke weed legally" I laughed… of course Brian did not. He kept right to the discussion.

"Yeah, they have stores, that you can just walk into and buy pot, you should come check it out" He invited.

"Is that where you are living these days?" I asked. "what happened to your house in North Phoenix"??

"I drive back and forth a lot" "My dog still lives out here, so I have to come home weekly". He explained.

"That's a lot of driving, man. How are you involved in the industry"? I inquired surprisingly. Brain never seemed like a pot type of guy.

"Well I hate to brag, but I've become one of the best growers in Los Angeles. In fact I can tell you, no one really produces the quality or quantity of product I can produce. Brian gloated. "The person who taught me, has been growing for 20 years. He gets only 2lbs per light set up. I get over 3 lbs and I'm on my 4th cycle.

"Man, I haven't smoked pot since college my friend" "not really something I'm interested in." "It was fun when I was young, but not worth the risk these days. Arizona is a zero tolerance state" I reminded.

"Oh, I have never smoked pot in my life" Brian responded. "I'm only in it for the money. You were telling me you were looking for an opportunity. What other opportunities are there right now?"

"Well ...you are in a growing industry" a slyly proclaimed. Brian's cold dark stare lightened a bit and he forced out a chuckle. Only to capture the sale... I am sure.

"Now Obama has promised to make it legal next year, so this is called being in the right place at the right time" The sales pitch continued. "You should think about getting involved."

"It just seems to strange to be true" I contorted." Hard to believe. No way Obamas gonna make it legal. Too many "sticks in the mud"" I just don't buy it." I proceeded.

"Well then come check it out for yourself" he challenged. "seeing is believing" Its only a couple hundred bucks to fly to LA. Beside you can use the vacation from boredom" " I can meet you at the airport so you won't even need to rent a car."

"Well I am bored shitless here, so I could fly out for a few days. Not a big deal. What are doing next week?" I inquired half heartedly.

"I'll be back in LA on Weds, you should come out then."

"Cool, I'll book a ticket on Expedia right now." I stated

"Cool" he mimicked.

"Oh, and one other thing I needed to ask you" sliding it in their as almost an afterthought.

"What is that?" I asked warily

"Do you think you could spot me $5k til January" he asked enthusiastically like we were already in business together.

Now this question hit me like a ton of bricks and came off as extremely odd. Here is this man, who has made millions of dollars, owns 3 houses,

Drives an SRT…and he wants to borrow money from me? This should have been my first red flag of things to come.

"UH…for what" I sputtered out, trying not to reveal my shock.

"well Lately, I've lost a lot of money. I got stuck upside down in a real estate deal for $800 k. In fact I'm almost bankrupt" He confessed. " I just need the money to buy some new grow equipment.I make 30 to 40 grand per yield, so I will have no problem paying you back with interest. In fact I will pay you back double in January, only two months from now."

"I'll have to think about it Brain" I replied. "I don't usually loan money to friends"

"OK", he sputtered in a nervous tone. "when will you know?" he continued to push.

"Give me a day or so" I assured. It still wasn't sitting good with me.

"Okay, I will call you tomorrow first thing" he continued. Oblivious to the situation." It's a good deal for you. You double your money in 2 months." It would be dumb to turn it down." Again he attempted a laugh which came out dry.

All of a sudden I felt uncomfortable having him in my house. I felt bad, but I didn't want to loan him the money. I just wanted the night to figure out how to politely say no. After another half an hour I announced I needed some sleep and escorted him to the door.

The next day was football Sunday. My Denver broncos were playing at 1 pm (expand) To cure my boredom, during half time, I had gotten in the habit of calling a girl off of craigslist. Nothing better than some bedroom action and football. I had also come to the realization that getting a girl off craigslist is a lot cheaper than getting a girlfriend and a whole lot more exciting. In the words of Charlie Sheen…"you don't pay them for sex…You pay them to go home, after sex". I decided to call the girl I had seen last week, named Erica. What her real name was... I'll probably never know. Now Erica was a soft spoken , blonde Bombshell of about 25 years of age. She lived in Anaheim CA but only worked in Arizona , so her family would never find out how she lived so well. They believed she was a model.

Last week, when I met her, my jaw honestly dropped to the floor. She was wearing a tied up , collared shirt with a red under garment, a short skirt and bobby sox. Her ample bosom revealed just enough to get you going and her legs were athletic, like the legs of a gymnast.

Now when you call a girl off Craigslist, you never really know what's going to show up at your door. Sometimes it's a cash and dash girl, who will let you get naked then slip out the door. It's never wise to follow them, because its almost guaranteed her driver/bouncer will be blocking her escape. Sometimes it's a crack whore that hadn't eaten in weeks and looked nothing like her former self in the photos.

It really was a roll of the dice...which honestly made it kind of exciting. A game of chance. But Erica was a pleasant surprise and truly enjoyed making men happy. Believe it or not, in this day and age, there are still women like that in this world. For $200 she was every man's 5 minute fantasy . I say 5 minutes because that's what Erica told me the average man lasts with her. I promised that would not be the case with me and she said good because she was really horny. We worked our way to the bedroom and I spent the next hour in heaven. I can tell she did not lie about being horny either.

Just as I was finishing her off, I heard a frantic knock on the door. I must say I was a little scared as maybe Erica had a pimp or something coming to move things along. She assured me she didn't however.

I went to the door …and low and behold, it was my new best friend Brian. What a buzz kill he was. I opened the door and he tried to work his way in to the house, but I stopped him.

"Brian, I'm not alone man. This isn't a good time" I told him, frankly.

"Oh, I thought we were meeting today" he said accusingly.

"No Brian, we were supposed to talk on the phone" I responded

"OK, but we need to decide what we are doing" "how long are you going to be? " he asked.

Now I wish I had just told him "No" at this point and it would have saved me years of this upcoming odyssey I'm about to recount to you.. But I told him I could meet him in an hour at the sports bar. He grinned and said ok. I closed the door and returned to by bedroom. Erica was now fully clothed and was just checking her makeup.

"Is everything ok "she asked.

"Whenever I get to see you everything is definitely ok" I promised, as a stared at her amazing firm body in disbelief.

Well I'm headed back to San Diego tonight, so text me in a couple weeks, if you want to see me again.

"Oh, I promise I want to see you again sexy. I can't wait. With that she gave me a peck on the cheek and strode towards door with a walk of pride on a job well done. Hips grinding into my memory. Our paths never crossed again, except for in my dreams…

So, I showed up to Dukes sports bar at about 12;00. Just enough time to get a table and order some food before the Broncos game came on. Arizona Cardinals were in the process of losing another game. No big surprise. At that time the local joke, in Arizona, for the cardinals was "come watch your favorite team beat the cardinals" and they were living up to that reputation again this year.

When Brian arrived, he wasn't interested in having a drink. He wanted to know if I knew any people who needed some weed.

"Brian I told you, I haven't done that in years man." "I don't hang out with those crowds any more" I reminded.

"I know he said, but everyone knows somebody" he came back with.

"Honestly Brian, I only know one couple who are very good friends that still smoke, Do you want me to call them? After the game?" I offered.

"Well, call them now, so we can go after the game if they are interested. I really need the money" red flag red flag… "please call them"

Alright but no guarantees I said. So my friends name was Shawn and he was from Australia. A couple of years earlier he had met his wife, through me, as she and I were really good friends at the time. I wasn't a hard conversation to have, so they invited me over to their home immediately after the game.

The game was uneventful with the Broncos dominating the Raiders, which was par for the course, so we didn't need to stay past the 3rd quarter. Brian offered to drive and I took him up on it for several reasons.

First of all, why should I waste my gas for his deal and second of all, if we got pulled over I wanted nothing to do with illegal drugs in my car. Now Brian drove a very nice BMW SUV of some sort. I'm not much of a car guy so we will leave it at that, but as soon as I entered the vehicle a familiar smell embraced me.

"Damn dude, you can get high just sitting in this car" I said. "what if you get pulled over? Your cooked if you do"

"No cops can't search your vehicle without probable cause" he promised.

"I don't know man but I think that your vehicle reeking of weed IS probable cause".

"No, they must have more than that, I've studied the law" he again promised.

My feeling was, not my car not my weed, not my problem. Then Brian started to drive. Now they say Asians are bad drivers but to be honest this is the first time I was ever actually in a car with one. He was so bad I actually feared for my life on several occasions. His speed was high, and he changed lanes often without signaling.

"Slow down cowboy' I demanded. You are carrying weed in this car remember. No sense pushing your luck." I reminded.

"he ha ha" he launched with out changing his speed or demeaner. He was driving to pick up cash and that all that mattered.

When we arrived at Shawn and stacys house, Brian went right to work grabbing a gym bag from the hatch of his vehicle. Shawn and Stacy met us at the door and brain nodded and walked right passed the to the kitchen table, barely saying hello.

Shawn and Stacy looked at me then looked at each other and I kind of shrugged it off. Brian will never be known as a people person. The Brain proceeded to pull out several large Tupperware containers and I mean the type you could store clothes in not food. There were 3 total and probably about 6 pounds in weight. Stacy glared at me as Shawn ran over to get a closer look. Again I shrugged. I had no idea of the quantity of pot he was carrying.

Brian cracked open the first container and the room quickly filled with a sweet sticky pineappley aroma. This is my Pineapple express he gleamed. Now I can tell you, this is the first time I had ever seen Brian genuinely smile. He was obviously proud of his product and ready to make a deal. Money was brains only passion. He lived for it. Everything else was a diversion.

Shawn had a glaze of excitement in his eyes as he creeped over to the containers. "bowls of paradise" he proclaimed not hiding his pleasure well. Stacy remained silent and distant. Silence for Stacy was unusual so I knew both me and Shawn were in for it later.

"Now what we have here is the best OG, that you will ever try" Brian exclaimed in a "Barnum and Bailey"step right up tone. Stacy remained cordial as she excused herself from the room. I also have Chemdog and Purple Kush if you like I can get it from y car" he offered.

A voice from the other room said" that's quite ok we don't need any-more weed in the house thank you" This is a Sheriff Joe size bust already" Stacy proclaimed. Her true feelings becoming known.

"How much do you want?" Brian asked Shawn.

"All of it" said Shawn with the look of pure pleasure in his eyes.

"I don't want you to get more than an OZ" the familiar voice from the other room demanded.

Shawn then realized his predicament so agreed with Stacy. "What is your price for an ounce he said.

"$450 for the OG and $350 for the rest" Brian announced.

"That's a pretty penny" Shawn replied. "I've never seen such variety."

Brian picked up a Bud the size of his small fist. He pulled out a mag-nifying glass from his bag.

"Let me show you something" he tempted. "see all those white crystals on the buds"

"Wow, Shane said, still amazed by the sheer quantity of the weed on his table.

"Those are the Tricombs" Brian continued, "That's what get s you the hallucinogenic effect."

"Looks like you sprinkled sugar on the weed" Shawn said laughingly.

"Yeah.he he ha" Brian faked another chuckle.

He handed me the magnifying glass. I had never seen anything like it either.

Now Shawn was very successful salesman with a large tech company so he didn't have problem picking up a couple ounces. No sooner did the money hit Brian's hands, that he started repacking his duffle and heading for the door. To say Brian lacked social skills is a major understatement. He tried to get Shawn number for future deliveries, but Shawn said just go through Dan in the future. I could tell even he had become nervous about these sheer quantity of flower.

Now I had had no idea this morning...that I was going to partake in an illegal drug deal. Oh well, a one time thing I thought. I must admit, once I realized how much pot was in the vehicle, I was nervous the rest of the way home and this time I demanded Brian obey the speed limits.

"Brian, can you slow it down a little man" I don't want either of us to get busted."

"ok ok " he complied. But his driving habits were still piss poor despite the speed drop.

"Drop me back at my house" I said Brian nodded.

When we arrived, I can't tell you how glad I was to be out of that vehicle. Note to self...never drive with

Brian again. End note.

Once we arrived, Brian started in about the loan again.

"So what did you decide about the money?" He pressured. "Can I borrow the $5000 for 2 months and you will double your money?"

"I'm still not sure Brian" I admitted.

"Welcome to California and I will convince you.' He assured. I will even show you where my grow is at ,so if I don't pay you back, that will be your insurance policy" he suggested. "after all, If I don't pay you back you can just report me to the police because I don't have a growers license." You could have me raided. You are in a "no lose" situation.

"I thought you said this was legal" I inquired

"It is legal, but police can still raid grows, right now. Growing permits haven't been established yet. This will change when Obama takes office" He assured.

"well I've already bought the plane ticket, so I guess we can talk about it more on Weds...In LA"

With that , Brian left.

I caught the end of the Sunday Night game. My bed still smelled of the delicious aroma of Erica's perfume. Damn that was a great start to the day. I fell asleep in front of the TV as usual.

Now "I've probably offended half the readers by admitting I enjoy the company of a paid provider every once in while Such a hypocritical society we live in. We broadcast sex all over the TV and all over our movies. We glorify it our music...but god forbid we actually have sex and enjoy it. In every city there are hundreds of massage parlors. Do you really think people need that many massages? The real joke is who is visiting them. Your local politician, your local police officer, your local pastor, your judges. Your holier than thou Christian. We still think we can take a totally normal and healthy human behavior and make it illegal. Sexual frustration of men Is probably a leading cause for murder and rape in this country. Relieving that frustration keeps us safer. By making it illegal we are making it more dangerous and expensive for all involved. What happens between and two consenting adults in the privacy of the bedroom is there own business. But that is a discussion for another book.

Chapter 3: On The Ground in Los Angeles
December 2008

B ack to the story for the lead-up to my big move to Los Angeles. Wednesday morning came quickly. My flight left Sky Harbor at 8:00 a.m. and landed an hour later. Once I hit the ground, I turned on my cell and texted Brian.

"The eagle has landed," I sent humorously.

"OK," came the unanimated response.

Carrying only a day pack, I headed straight for the exit and saw Brian in front of a metallic-colored SUV. As soon as he saw me, he headed right to the driver's door with barely a "hello." As I opened the passenger door and jumped in, I was hit again by the sticky-sweet aroma.

"Damn, dude. You need to mask that smell. It reeks of pot in here," I complained.

"Really?" he asked, surprised. "I guess I'm just used to it."

"If you get pulled over, man, the cops are gonna smell it," I promised.

He asserted his theory of probable cause to search a vehicle. I later discovered a police dog represents a probable cause, so if an officer smells it, he just needs to call the K-9 unit.

"Just drive careful, man. This is LA, and I sure as hell don't want to go to jail here."

"OK," he agreed.

"Where are we going first?" I asked.

"I have someone I want you to meet. He's a retired attorney who can explain all the laws to you…then we will go to my grow," he said with pride. Rarely did I see Brian smile, but I could tell he was really proud of his growing prowess.

"All right," I said.

I had forgotten my promise to never ride with Brian again. Here I found myself in LA with LA drivers. Oh my God, what had I done…

We continued around LAX, looking for the exit to the 405. As soon as we jumped on the 405, there was the gridlock traffic for which LA is famous. I had heard about the traffic, but you have to see it to believe it really. Nonstop cars as far as the eye can see.

"I don't know how people do this every day, Brian. How can you live in this urban concrete jungle with all this traffic?"

"You get used to it," he explained.

Just then, a police cruiser's lights came on right behind us. My heart jumped through my head. I looked at Brian, and his eyes were intently looking into the rearview mirror. The cruiser zipped into a passing lane and whizzed right by us.

"Must be an accident," Brian surmised, without emotion.

"I'm nervous already. How much pot do you have in the car right now?"

"About six pounds," he responded.

I just sank into my seat and wondered what I had gotten myself into.

"Just drive cool, man. I've never been arrested, and I don't want to start today."

"OK," Brian assured me.

In my mind, I was kicking myself for coming to LA in the first place. I made a mental note: "I'm definitely *not* moving to LA."

After forty-five minutes of bumper-to-bumper traffic, we finally exited the 405 into a suburb called Van Nuys.

"There is a large Asian community living here," Brian explained. It was obvious by all the Vietnamese restaurants and massage parlors.

We soon arrived at a small coffee shop and began looking for parking. That was a twenty-minute endeavor in itself. We finally located a spot, halfway into a residential neighborhood. Brian stowed his GPS in the glove compartment, then exited the vehicle. I jumped out of the car and waited for him on the sidewalk.

Brian reignited our conversation from forty-five minutes ago. He must have been thinking about it and the police cruiser the entire time.

"Even if we got pulled over, the cops couldn't take my product," he explained. "I'm a patient with a valid doctor's recommendation and a state ID."

I didn't know enough about it to argue.

"In fact, a guy was just in court last week. Seems the police had caught him with sixty pounds and confiscated it. The judge ordered the police to return it immediately."

"Wow. It's a different world than where I come from," I said in disbelief.

"Mark will explain everything," he promised.

The coffee shop had an outdoor patio with only a few tables occupied. Brian walked directly to the table with a man and a dog sitting at it. The man smiled excitedly and stood up as he saw us approaching.

"Hey, Mark," Brian said. "I want you to meet a friend of mine—Dalton."

Mark looked at me with a relaxed smile and an outstretched hand. "Welcome to LA," he said as we shook hands.

My first impression of Mark was that he looked very tired. He was an older man, possibly in his early sixties, with a slender frame. His skin had a paleness to it, his handshake was feeble, and his hand was somewhat cold to the touch. His voice was weak but confident.

"So how was your flight?" he said, continuing with the typical ice-breaking questions.

"Non-eventful," was the usual response to the usual question.

"Just the way you want it to be," he chided. "Would you like a coffee or something?"

"No, I'm good," I replied. I had been up since 5:30 a.m. and already had enough caffeine in my system.

"Have a seat," he invited as he motioned toward the chairs. As I pulled out the chair, his dog, a tired, overweight golden retriever, stood up to sniff my leg and check out my groin area. I extended my hand to the dog so he could get a good sniff.

"What's the dog's name?" I inquired.

"Butch," he replied, obviously proud of his long-time companion. "Don't be a pest, Butch," he scolded.

"Oh, don't worry; I like dogs. He's just checking me out," I observed.

"So Brian tells me you've been business associates for many years," he said.

"Yeah, we've known each other for a while," I replied.

"What questions can I answer for you?" he offered.

"Well, Brian told me you were the medical marijuana expert here in Los Angeles. I'm just here to explore the opportunity. It's all very new and overwhelming, quite honestly."

"OK, so let me give you a little background on the situation," he said as he took a small sip from his coffee. "Back in 1996, California passed the California Compassionate Care Act, also known as Prop 215. Since this was passed as a voter initiative, only another voter's initiative can reverse it.

No judge's orders or legislative act can interfere with it. Prop 215, in a nutshell, allows people to grow and distribute marijuana to medical patients who have a recommendation from a doctor. The guidelines were then confirmed in Senate Bill 420 by the California legislature. Now, this can be only done from patient to patient or through a group of patients known as a collective. Since that time, literally thousands of storefronts have popped up across the state."

"What would qualify you to be a patient?" I asked, still believing this was just a California scheme to smoke pot legally.

"You would be amazed," he said. "Marijuana is truly a miracle drug. It's used for glaucoma patients, AIDS, and even cancer. It helped me keep my appetite through my chemotherapy. I couldn't keep anything down without it," he explained.

That explained his feeble look, I noted. I began to let my defenses down somewhat with this revelation.

"Maybe there is something to this," I conceded in my mind.

"Brian tells me you're a pretty astute businessman," he said, stroking my ego. Brian would never have said that.

"I've done well," I bragged.

"The key to success in this industry is, first of all, to find a partner you can trust. Second, to run it like a business and follow the guidelines to the letter of the law. Unfortunately, there are too many young stoners out there, opening up shops and giving the industry a bad name. We could use more businessmen like yourself to legitimize the industry."

"So what is your incentive to help us?" I inquired. "Brian tells me you're an attorney?"

"I'm retired from practicing law. I just have a real passion for the subject. Basically, you hire me as a consultant for a flat fee of $3,500, and I will guide you through the process. The first thing we would need to do is find a location. Once you have a location, we need to get you a hardship application. After that, I can introduce you to whoever you wish to meet to get you up and running. Luckily for you, you already have an incredible grower in Brian."

Brian chimed in about his quality. "Yeah, I sell my product at the high-end clubs here in LA. In fact, The Farmacy buys everything I produce."

"What's The Farmacy?" I asked.

"It's a high-end, boutique-style store over on Lincoln Boulevard in the Venice Beach area. They have three stores. I'll take you to one tomorrow," he promised.

"So the bottom line is to find a location, retain your mark, and we are in business," I summarized.

"Yep, I'll be with you throughout the process," he promised.

"How much money can we make?" I asked, getting down to the most important question of all.

"The sky's the limit," Mark said. "Most clubs clear over a million per year. With your business sense, you could double or triple that." He was stroking my ego once again.

"We will be like China," Brian said. "We will be producing all our own goods."

That statement made no sense, but I let it go.

"I'll be honest, it would take a lot to convince me to move to LA. I've still got to think about this *a lot*," I reminded them.

"I think when you go to The Farmacy, you will be convinced," Mark said.

"We will see…I guess so," I said, trying to hide my growing excitement.

"Let me give you my card," Mark offered as he pulled out a gold card case, with a pot leaf etched into the cover. "Call me with any questions you might have. I'm always available."

"I will," I promised.

"Very good," I said as I stood up and accepted the card. Brian followed my lead, and we shook Mark's hand and then made our way back to the SUV. Butch raised his head slightly and then laid back down as we left.

"Where to next?" I asked.

"We have to go to my grow site. I have to meet some guys there."

"Is it far?" I asked.

"With LA traffic, it will take over an hour," he estimated.

"Hmm," I thought to myself. My whole life I had avoided traffic situations, and now here I was smack dab in the middle of the gridlocked capital city...Bummer.

Sure enough, as soon as we got on the ramp, I saw five lanes of traffic bumper to bumper. At least now I was a little more excited about being here.

An hour turned into two hours as the lunch-hour traffic was heavy. Finally, again we exited, but this time into a small hilly community named Hedena, I think.

It looked like every other dirty, rundown street I had seen in LA thus far, with gas stations, 7-Elevens, and shopping plazas. We drove about two miles down the main drag and into a very small parking lot next to a small building with bars on the windows.

"This is it?" I asked, very unimpressed.

"Yeah," Brian responded. "Wait here."

He hopped out of the car and walked around the building. He came back, then grabbed his phone and sent a text.

"They will be here soon," he said.

"Who will?" I asked.

"My construction guys that built out this grow. Come with me."

He pulled two empty duffle bags out of his truck and slung them over his shoulder.

"Watch your step," he cautioned as we rounded the corner. We were on a narrow sidewalk crossed by weeds on each side. There was no light, so I could barely make out Brian's small form in front of me.

"Hold these," he commanded, as he slid the duffle bags off his shoulders and pushed them my way.

"Wait here," he commanded again as he unlocked a series of deadbolts on the security doors. Beyond the door was a stronger steel door with more deadbolts.

"Damn, no one is breaking in here," I exclaimed.

"Nope, the ceiling is what I worry about," Brian explained.

Once the steel door was opened, Brian entered a code into the keypad. A small beep indicated the security alarm was deactivated.

"Close the door behind you and lock it," he added. I did as I was instructed. Brian was already moving down the hallway, so I followed. Inside, I was still unimpressed. It was a very small room, with old furniture, no décor, and unfinished walls. Honestly, the building needed to be condemned.

"Got a bathroom?" I asked eagerly, after the long drive.

"Over there." He motioned to a small doorway. The bathroom was dirty and dark.

"The light is out," Brian explained.

I did my best to hit the target, listening for water at the base of the toilet as I unleashed my coffee from much earlier in the day. I came back to the main room, and Brian motioned for me to follow him. He opened a nearby door, and a radiant light gleamed from inside. I had never seen such a bright light inside a building. It seemed as bright as the sun. As I stepped inside the room, a blast of heat hit my face and arms.

"Close the door," Brian barked. I found myself surrounded, in tight quarters, by a sea of green plants maybe three to four feet high. The lights above them hung from chains, just inches from the tops of the plants. There were fans strategically placed throughout the room, aimed at the lights. A distinct smell filled my nostrils, bringing back memories of those long summer days in high school.

"Wow," I said. "Now I'm impressed."

Whenever Brian talked about his plants, his whole demeanor changed. A definite pride and confidence overtook his normally expressionless face.

"These are my babies," he said, his face glowing in the high-powered lights.

"Does it have to be so hot in here?" I asked, wondering how anyone could work in this environment.

"The lights put off a lot of heat," he said. "Actually, I have an air conditioner running to cool the room down," he explained.

"Wow, that must kill the electric bill," I said.

"Yeah, it was $2,000 last month," he confirmed.

"And that's how the cops get you," he added. "They look for spikes in electric bills so they know you are growing marijuana. Luckily, this building is attached to a machine shop so high electric bills are normal."

"What is the big tank right there?" I asked, trying to understand the setup.`

"That's for reverse osmosis of the water," he explained. "They can't just get regular water; the PH is too high."

He continued, "The water is stored in this tank, then a timer waters every twenty-four hours. See these large pans under the plants? They fill with water, then drain. You don't want to overwater either. The whole system is called hydroponics."

"Quite a detailed operation," I said as I admired.

"Yeah, you really need to know what you are doing." Brian beamed with pride. "I produce the best OG in LA," he boasted.

"OG?" I inquired.

"Yeah, it's called the Original Gangster. I guess it's Snoop Dog's favorite."

"Smell this bud," he offered.

I took the bud from him, and the first thing I noticed was a sticky residue. The smell was intense—very sweet.

"I cannot judge its quality until I smoke some," I teased, with an almost straight face.

"Oh, that's not ready to smoke yet," he said, not even noticing the joke. "That's got two more weeks, then it's got to cure," he explained.

"Cure?" I asked. "Back in the day, we would just spread something out on a Frisbee and separate out the seeds, then roll a big one," I said with a grin.

"Oh, there are no seeds," he said. "These are grown from clones. No one has seeds anymore."

"Good because one time I was driving down the road with a friend, smoking a big one, and a seed exploded. A few minutes later, my stoned friend announced my shirt was on fire…"

My story was cut short by Brian's phone ringing.

"Yeah," Brian said with his usual charm. "OK; wait a minute," he said.

He squeezed his way back through the pungent branches of weed and instructed me to open the door. As I opened the door, I was greeted by the coolness of the main room. I hadn't noticed the sweat that had accumulated on my neck until the fan hit me. Brian told me to wait here, then proceeded to the front door. Ten minutes turned to twenty, and Brian hadn't returned. Slowly, the gravity of the situation started weighing on me. Here I was standing in a drug house, somewhere in Los Angeles. What if Brian was being robbed or arrested? I was just sitting here like a dumbass either way.

I started to make my way to the door when I heard the latch click. It was Brian, followed by a very large man and his smaller companion. I made my way out of the narrow hallway to the main room. Brian had a nervous look on his face as he introduced me.

"This is Rob and Steve," he said. Rob stretched out his large hand. You could tell the guy did some serious bodybuilding, along with some steroids.

"Hey," he said quickly.

Steve was much smaller, with kind of a "surfer hippy dude" look. Long blond curls came from under his black ski cap. He seemed more cordial than Rob and offered some small talk as the two started unpacking their tools.

"They're here to fix a ballast that I have been having problems with," Brian explained.

Rob made his way to the plant room, with Steve right behind him. Brian followed, but I opted not to go in. First of all, having four people in that small room was about three people too many, and, second, I was enjoying the cooler air outside of it.

"I'll wait out here," I volunteered. No one acknowledged me. After ten minutes or so, Steve came back out.

"There. Almost done," he said.

"Let me show you the baby room," he offered as he walked to a door on the other side, which I had not noticed earlier.

As he opened the door, the same radiant light hit his face. I stood at the doorway as he patiently nurtured the "baby plants," as he called them.

"How much do you know about growing?" he asked as he continued to handle the plants tenderly.

"Absolutely nothing," I confessed, feeling inadequately stupid at that moment. "I'm just the business guy," I explained, trying to make myself seem valuable.

"Good, there are too many kids in this business without any business savvy. They're ruining it for everyone in my opinion." I thought it was an odd comment since he couldn't have been more than two years old himself.

"He's got mites," Steve proclaimed with disgust, as he intentionally viewed the undersides of the babies. "Damn it. I told him to get ladybugs. See these little white bumps on the underside of the leaves?"

I looked, trying to see what he was talking about.

"Brian!" he shouted to the other room. "Come here."

After a few seconds, Brian emerged from the doorway, with Rob directly behind him. When he got to the baby room, Steve seemed very annoyed.

"Did you use that pesticide, like I told you not to do?" he asked sarcastically.

"Yeah, it works," Brian assured him.

"No, Brian, it doesn't work. I told you to get ladybugs. They eat the mites and the eggs. The spray only works on the mites, not the eggs. You're gonna lose your whole crop if you don't listen to me," Steve scolded.

Rob, who was towering over Brian's right shoulder, reaffirmed what Steve had just said.

"When we tell you to do something, Brian, just do it," Rob said. The veins in his neck protruded with disgust and anger. His hands were clenched, as if ready to pound Brian to a pulp.

Now, I was trying to sort everything out in my head without enough information, but the situation did take me by surprise. Quite frankly, I didn't understand why, if this was Brian's grow, his building, and his investment, these people were so angry. It seemed like there must be more to the story. I decided to keep my mouth shut but would have had no problem getting involved if things got physical. I've always enjoyed a good fight and thought the meathead would go down pretty easily. Both Steve and Brian seemed inconsequential.

"How can I get ladybugs?" Brian asked Steve, avoiding Rob's stare.

"I'll get some for you," Steve said. "You just need to listen."

"OK," Brian promised. The look on Rob's face eased a little, and the veins retracted back into his trunk-like neck.

"We're done here," Rob announced. "When are you gonna have our money?" he added in a threatening tone.

"The crop should be ready in three weeks," Brian promised.

"Then you will still have to cure it," Steve reminded him. "That will take three more weeks."

"True," Brian agreed, still avoiding Rob's glare. "But I already have it sold, so no worries," he said with a nervous giggle.

"Yeah, but if these spider mites wipe out your whole crop because you didn't listen, then how are you gonna pay us?" Steve asked.

"You need to fucking listen, Brian," he threatened. "I'm tired of telling you that."

It all started to make more sense now. Brian owed them money. Got it.

With that, Rob and Steve walked to the door, slinging their tools on their shoulders.

"Nice meeting you," said Steve.

"Later," said Rob. As they turned, I sized up Rob's massive biceps and back.

"Yeah, I could take him," I surmised. I had always felt a little protective of my friends ever since high school and had gotten in many fights because of it, usually with much larger guys. Being the captain of my wrestling team back in the day taught me how to use size and weight against an opponent. I had little tolerance for disrespect.

With that, however, they made their way into the darkness. Brian closed the door and latched it behind them.

"Let me water the plants and then we can go," Brian said.

I looked at my cell phone and noticed it was past midnight. It had been a long and interesting day, to say the least.

"Yeah, I need to get some sleep tonight," I told Brian as he reentered the radiant room.

"Just fifteen minutes," he promised.

I stood in the empty room, checking my text messages and surfing the web on my phone. There was an old wooden chair that didn't seem too sturdy, so I elected to lean against the corresponding wooden table instead. Thirty-five minutes later, I peeked into the room.

"Are you ready?" I asked.

Brian looked up and explained he had been having a time issue, but that it was now resolved. He exited the room, then said he had to do one more thing. He grabbed a spray bottle from the bathroom, filled it with liquid from a jug under the table, then walked to the baby room.

"This stuff works great; I don't care what they say," he said as he began to douse the plants.

"They seemed totally pissed," I reminded him.

"Nah, they are always like that. I get better yield than they do, and I'm not letting ladybugs in here. They're a mess and just escape anyway. They are not cheap either," he explained.

This info was all Greek to me. I didn't have a clue who was right.

Once Brian was finished with the babies, he grabbed some jars of pot he had stowed in the closet.

"You keep it in glass jars?" I asked.

"Yeah, they cure better in glass," he explained.

I took his word for it, as I was getting tired. This forty-five-year-old body wasn't usually up past 10:00 p.m., let alone midnight.

As we got in the SUV, Brian explained, "I have to pick up the taxi until my first crop comes in."

"You're gonna stay up all night?" I asked.

"Only until six, then I'll sleep until 3:00 p.m. and start over."

"Crazy," I thought. "How the mighty have fallen." This man was driving a taxi just to pay his bills.

"What's on the agenda for tomorrow?" I asked.

"I'm going to take you to some pot shops, so you can see I'm not full of shit."

"OK, but do I have to wait until 3:00 pm? Remember, I don't know anyone here," I stated.

"What time do you want to meet then?" he asked.

"How about noon?" I suggested.

"OK," Brian conceded.

We drove through the night streets, jumped on the highway, then exited into another residential neighborhood. After winding through some poorly lit streets, we arrived at a duplex, with a yellow taxi parked in the drive.

"I've got to feed the dog," he explained. "I'll be back in a second."

He made his way to the house and I started to follow, but he turned and told me to stay put.

"My dog doesn't like people," he warned. More waiting.

Brian was gone for a very short time, and then we loaded the bags into the trunk of the cab and drove a half hour to my hotel in Van Nuys. The city seemed huge to me. I had no idea where I was or where I was going. I had to put total trust in Brian. That idea started to worry me. It was 2:00 a.m. when we finally got to the hotel.

"You want a little bud to check the quality?" he asked.

I thought, "What the heck? I'm on vacation and doing some research, right? Why not." So I accepted.

"I don't have a pipe or papers," I said, hoping he did.

"Just use an apple or a toilet paper roll," he suggested, as I stepped out of the car. The sad part is…I knew exactly what he was talking about.

"See you at noon," I reminded him.

As I walked to my room, I wondered where the hell I was going to find an apple at 2:00 a.m. As I checked in, I saw a soda machine in the lobby.

"That will work," I thought to myself as I grabbed the keys from the night clerk. When I got to the room, I eagerly emptied the contents of the can into the toilet. I pulled out my steel point pen from my pocket and punched small holes into one side of the can, forming a bowl and creating a screen of sorts.

"I guess high school is finally paying off," I laughed to myself.

I grabbed the bud out of my pocket and crushed it on the nightstand. I removed the stem and separated the flower into a neat little pile. I loaded the bowl, lit a match, and began to caress the flame into the goodies in the bowl.

I felt the smoke hit my lungs and coughed violently without notice. The content of the bowl spread onto the bedspread, with the hot cherry and all. Quickly, I set the can down and beat out the smoldering ashes. The comforter had a small burn hole in it, the size of a dime.

"I guess it has been a while," I thought.

As I viewed the mess of ashes on the floor, my mind and body began to float. A smile eased across my face as I reached for the bowl again. This time, my lungs were fully prepared, and I took a deep hit and held it in. Relaxation filled my entire body. After a minute, I let out a stream of smoke and laid back in bed.

"Now that's better," I said to an empty room. A sense of euphoria took over.

Now, if you have never been stoned, all your cares and worries seem to leave you as you exhale. Seemingly simple tasks and occurrences become intriguing. Thoughts you haven't thought in twenty years come back to you. Dreams that died decades ago have new life breathed into them. Sensations that have dulled over time are new and crisp. Apples taste better, showers cascade over you in slow motion, and sex seems like an encounter with the gods. Every touch, every kiss has meaning...

I was awoken rudely by a blaring alarm clock at 7:00 a.m. I awoke to find the room just how I had left it. The TV had run throughout the night, invading my dreams with whatever happened to be on the screen. I had distant memories of the ShamWow guy trying to taunt me through the imaginary world of fantasy mixed with reality.

"I really need to set the sleep time next time," I thought to myself. ShamWow is not my idea of restful sleep.

With five hours to kill, I decided to hop in the shower and head down for breakfast. As I got dressed, the temptation to smoke another bowl crept into my head.

"Nope. No way," I told myself. "You need to be clearheaded today as you evaluate this opportunity." So I made a small envelope out of hotel stationery and carefully stowed my newly acquired treasure in it for a later time.

I had forgotten how freeing pot was. I was much more relaxed than I had been for quite some time, but now my brain was stuck on stupid.

"That's OK," I thought, as it was going to be a laid-back day anyway.

Continental breakfast was served in a room by the front desk in the lobby area, so I gorged myself on cereals, fruit, toast, and coffee. The coffee was dark and strong and cut through the murky stupidity of the lingering effects of the bud.

After one too many cups, I got the jitters as I walked back to my room.

"Damn coffee," I thought, chuckling to myself. "I should have stuck with the peaceful stupidity of the plant."

It's truly amazing to me how misled everyone is about the effect of marijuana. I'm sure, if you are trying to relax, most people would choose its effects over coffee, cigarettes, or alcohol. I don't recommend it if you are studying for the bar exam, but some people excel with it.

In fact, during my last year in college, I was studying calculus and just couldn't quite get it. I spoke with a friend who was a few years ahead of me in engineering, and he agreed to tutor me. The very first night, I went over to his apartment, he wanted to show me his "closet project."

Inside the closet was a four-foot plant, complete with lighting and the works. He explained the cycles of the plant to me and how he was perfecting his craft. We then went to the kitchen table. He loaded up a bowl, took a big drag, and offered it to me.

"You can smoke pot and do calculus?" I asked as I politely rejected his offer.

"Absolutely," he said. "My thinking becomes more creative when I'm high."

"Not me, man. I would just want to curl up on the couch and eat Doritos, so no thanks," I laughed.

Once he was sufficiently stoned, he amazed me with his comprehension of the subject and explained it so simply that even I could understand it.

Brian arrived at my hotel at about 2:00 p.m. He explained he had eaten a "brownie" and overslept.

"A medicated brownie?" I asked. "I thought you didn't partake?"

"Oh, I take edibles; I just don't smoke," he responded.

Being late was typical of Brian, I was soon to learn.

We drove to an area in Venice Beach and to a store called The Farmacy on Abbot Kinney Boulevard. It was a large, very attractive, high-end establishment with the doors standing wide open. The woodwork inside gave it the look and feel of a fine cigar shop.

An armed security guard stood by the left side of the door, and a greeting podium was to the right. An attractive, hippie-looking girl in her twenties welcomed us as we walked into the lobby. She wore a flowery dress and had a small nose ring. Her dress was made of a light material and barely covered her slim, if not skinny, body. She also sported a tattoo on one of her uncovered shoulders of a skull and a rose. "Hmm" was my only thought.

"Welcome to The Farmacy," she said, acknowledging us. "Are your returning members?"

"I'm returning," Brian said as he pulled out his membership card.

"OK, sign in," she said, as she handed a registration book to Brian.

"And you, sir?" she asked, with pleasant but serious eyes.

"Oh, I'm with him," I explained.

"Then you will have to wait here," she said. "This area is only for members."

"No worries," I said. I grabbed a chair near the door that faced the retail space. The room was alive with interesting smells of incense, baked goods, and, of course, ganja. To the right of me was a clerk behind a glass counter. Several wooden shelves were stocked behind him with the familiar glass jars.

All the jars were labeled with interesting names, such as Maui Wowie, Grape Ape, Jack Herrer, and others. There were about forty jars in all. I couldn't believe my eyes.

Customers were lined up in front of the counter, where a small-framed, Jamaican-looking guy was opening the jars one by one for the members to inspect and smell. When the customer found something pleasing, Jamaican Bob, as I nicknamed him, would weigh out the quantity, insert it into what looked like a pill container, and collect the money. I could not get over the fact that we were literally twelve feet from the curbside of the street, in plain view of passersby and the police. All of them could witness a marijuana transaction.

"My, how the world is changing," I thought.

As I surveyed the room again, I noticed several stand-up coolers, like the kind you see at 7-Eleven, lined up along the left wall. Inside, I could see a variety of bottled drinks, but none of them appeared to be Coke or Pepsi products. One had the distinctive emblem of a pot leaf on the label. In front of the coolers was another counter, but this had some chest coolers below it, like the kind you might see used for ice cream. To the right of the counter, I saw a variety of baked goods. There were brownies and muffins and what looked to be some type of banana bread, sold by the slice. In the glass window was a warning label, stating, "Warning: These edibles contain THC and are not recommended for consumption before driving or operating heavy machinery."

"Wow," I thought. "It's a stoner's Walmart."

To the back of the room, there was a series of shelves, stretching to the ceiling, holding every type of bong you could ever want.

Wait, did I just write bong? God, do you realize people have actually been arrested for calling it a bong? Don't believe me? Look it up! Tommy Chong did time in prison for advertising "bongs." You see, what I was about to learn over the next few months is that in California, the Feds act like it's a communist country in many ways, as will be discussed in future chapters. Yes, you can be arrested for using the wrong words. The proper word is "water pipe." And don't you forget it!

Anyway, at the very top of the shelves, I could see hookahs lavishly decorated with many brilliantly colored laces hanging down their sides. To the right of the shelves, I noticed a small stairway, perhaps three steps high, going to a door. To the right of the door was a dark window. Behind the window, I could see the silhouette of a rather large man.

"That's the real security," I thought to myself. I looked again at the street. "Amazing. It's about time," I thought with a smile.

Just then, a little old lady appeared in the doorway. She was sitting in one of those electric wheelchairs and had a variety of tubes going toward her head and mouth. She had a sweet look on her face, and her eyes looked excited as she surveyed the room. She drove her chair to the security guard, with a piece of paper in her hand. He directed her over to the check-in counter.

The young lady welcomed her with unbridled enthusiasm and took the piece of paper from her hand. From what I could overhear, she was a new patient. The young lady, whose name was Bree according to her name tag, asked the older lady to wait as she verified the information. The older lady seemed to make small sounds without actually speaking. Bree then went over to her computer and picked up the phone.

"Yes, I am calling to confirm a patient by the name of Margaret Myers, number 12472472, expiration date December 22, 2010," Bree said.

Once confirmed, Bree went to the printer on her left and pulled out the newly printed paper. Then Bree proceeded to encase the paper into a plastic sheath of some sort.

"You're all set, Margaret," Bree announced gleefully, as she approached the older lady, who was positioned right next to me.

"Come with me," Bree encouraged as she motioned to Margaret to enter the main room. The lady smiled and followed Bree as instructed.

Once in the room, Bree stopped in front of the wheelchair and bent over, facing the lady. Being a typical guy, I admired her slender legs as the dress lifted a bit. There was also a large tattoo adorning her upper left thigh, facing directly at me. It seemed to be a picture of some type of goddess or female ghost, but the face was covered by the bottom of her short dress.

"I sure wouldn't mind seeing the rest of that tattoo," I thought to myself in eager anticipation.

"What can I show you today?" Bree asked, with genuine enthusiasm.

The lady whispered something, which caused Bree to move closer, so as to hear her. After another attempt at communicating her needs, Bree seemed to understand and walked back to the counter with Jamaican Bob.

Now, Bob acted slightly annoyed by this intrusion into his space and from the looks of him and his demeanor, he looked like he might be in outer space right then and there. Probably perma-stoned.

Bree mentioned for Bob to notice "Maggie" in the wheelchair, so Bob reluctantly stepped aside and allowed Bree to serve her. Bree motioned to the lady to come forward by passing some of Bob's customers.

Bree pulled down several jars and began opening each one. She seemed to tell a story about each jar and then would hand Maggie a large bud in the vial for her inspection. Now, remember these were the "Wild West" days of medical marijuana so back then you could actually touch the weed. Not very sanitary, I must say. A lot has changed in only a few short years.

Maggie would attempt to hand the vial back, but being constrained to the chair, she needed help. Luckily a patient behind her assisted her to get the vial back on the counter. After two more vials were inspected, the lady pointed at one of the jars, and the decision was made. Bree's face lit up when Maggie had made her choice. She closed the other two jars and returned them to the shelf. She then grabbed the chosen jar and walked to a scale situated on the back counter. She meticulously weighed the product and put some back in the jar at some point. Presumably, she had overweighed some. With that, the flower was put into the medical vials, labeled, and bagged.

"We also have a free gift for you as a first-time visitor," she said, slipping a preroll into the bag.

Just then, Brian appeared from around the corner. "Let's go," he said as he walked to the exit. Out on the street, Brian seemed jovial.

"What did you think?" he asked, knowing the answer.

"Holy shit, dude. I still can't believe it," I responded.

"Two of my strains are there on the top shelf," he bragged again. "Just think about it, man. We could have our own store and bypass them. We would be like China with really good prices. We would also have the best bud on the planet. No one could touch us."

"It's something to think about," I agreed, trying to conceal my true feelings of excitement. We walked half a block past a small café on Abbot Kinney.

"You hungry?" I asked.

"Sure," Brian responded as we grabbed an outdoor table. "What other business can we start with such high demand and such a low overhead?" he asked.

"In this economy, nothing," I agreed.

"I've already got a name picked out for our store. The Bakery," he announced, all proud. "Get it? Get baked at the bakery?"

"Uh ok," I said. I was obviously not as excited as he was about the name.

Being an entrepreneur for the last twenty years, I did realize that there's no such thing as a bad idea, so I played along with this one. "Yeah, we could have all the employees wear chef's hats," I joked playfully.

"Yeah, I guess," Brian said, a bit confused and not getting the joke.

"I still have a lot of thinking to do before I can make this decision. I'm not thrilled about living in this concrete jungle," I reminded him.

"It's not so bad," he promised. "There are tons of pretty women here."

"I've noticed that," I agreed, "and such variety. I've seen Asian, Black, Latina, and Persian women. I've seen quite a few exotic mixes as well. Black/Asian Asian/Hispanic. So many women, so little time."

"These girls are not your typical California bleached blondes that you see on TV," he stated. "And much different from Phoenix for sure." Uh oh, Brian knew my weak spot...

"So how about the loan?" he asked again. "It's only until January, so it's three months and then you double your money," he promised. "Now you know where my grow is, so if I don't pay you, you can shut me down."

"That's not my goal, Brian," I replied. Little did I know, at the time, this exact information would be needed and used in the future to secure my rights and investment.

"But it's good security," he again emphasized.

"I probably will," I said. Just need a few more days to think about it.

"When can you let me know?" he kept pushing.

"Give me until Monday," I replied. "I will give you a definite yes or no then."

"Now get me to the airport," I demanded. "My flight leaves in a few hours and if the airport is anything like the highways here...I'm already late." We consumed our sandwiches and headed for the door.

With that, we paid our bill and walked toward the car. Again, I had to cover Brian's weak tip, as he never left anything for the server. I hadn't known many Asians in my life, but this one was a cheap ass, even when he had money.

"No big deal," I thought. "His problem, not mine."

44

As suspected, traffic was thick heading down Venice Boulevard.

"What a mess," I thought.

At one traffic light, we had to wait for three greens just to get through it. In my mind, I kept weighing the pros and cons of moving to LA. The business model was intriguing for sure. The weather was great. The women were stunning, but traffic and prices were horrible.

"I guess you have to take the bad with the good," I surmised.

The airport was no better. Luckily, I only flew with a carry-on. Still, the line to get through security was horrendous. Not the pinnacle of efficiency. Sky Harbor was much better, I thought. I was halfway through the security screening when a shocking thought came to mind.

"I still have the marijuana in my possession," I realized in horror.

"Shit," I thought. I jumped out of line and raced to the bathroom. Inside the stall, I emptied the small quantity into the toilet, then flushed. I threw the bag in the trash can as I exited the washroom.

The line had grown in length.

"How could I have been so stupid?" I chastised myself. I gave myself the benefit of the doubt, however. After all, it had been a good twenty years since I had possessed this "narcotic."

Still, I couldn't shake the thought of how quickly my life could have changed by such a stupid mistake. With marijuana, the punishment far outweighed the crime, as many young men and women were finding out. Our government was willing to ruin a person's life over a plant—a plant, for God's sake. In the words of the late, great Jack Herrer, "Someday, the government is going to owe us a big damn apology." I wouldn't hold your breath.

I had never been arrested and wanted to keep it that way.

Finally, I got to my plane, found my seat, and settled back for the trip. I ordered a couple of Jack-and-Cokes for the short 45-minute flight. Still my drug of choice, I thought, as I napped the rest of the way.

Chapter 4: Decision Time

O nce back home, I spent the next couple of days contemplating the opportunity. Over the weekend, I called up an ex-business partner and invited him to lunch. I have found, when facing a big decision, it is useful to get a third-party opinion. It had to be someone with business savvy. Not an attorney or a family member. They can only give information from a jaded perspective. An attorney will tell you all the bad things that could happen. Most can't even run their own business, much less mine. A family member is only concerned about your safety and proximity to them for holiday events.

Donald Smith and I had been partners for over six years in the Adventure Club business, back in 1999. He was more or less a silent partner but had good business sense. He tended to think more about the profit portion of things, whereas I was more focused on the challenges and obstacles of a new venture.

I always believed, and still do, that I have a distinct advantage over my competitors. Why? Because I truly understand the value of word of mouth and customer service better than anyone.

Sure, everyone talks about the value of word-of-mouth advertising, but when you ask them how it works, they come up with nothing.

My answer is this: When a customer comes into my area, I want it to be an experience—something they won't forget two minutes after leaving the store. To achieve this, you must touch as many senses as possible. Touch, smell, sight, sounds, and taste, as well as emotions like humor,

respect, gratitude, appreciation, excitement, satisfaction, and intrigue…
You want them to "experience" your store and your staff. Not just visit.

Donald, who was ten years my senior, admired my ability to build a
business from the ground up. Our last business I had built to over a million dollars per year on a $4,000 loan.

When Donald and I met at the Denny's for lunch, I could not wait
to get his feedback. Now, Donald was somewhat more conservative than
I was. For his day job, he was a commercial airline pilot, which kept him
out of town about fifteen days per month. On his off days, he dabbled in
different business ideas.

We followed the waitress to the booth, and both ordered a cup of coffee. The waitress returned immediately to fill our cups and take the order.
Once the order was placed, I got right down to the topic at hand. I really
wasn't quite sure what my straight-laced conservative friend would say. I
think I was hoping he would talk me out of it.

"So what do you know about medical marijuana?" I jumped right in
with the question.

"Not much; I hear it's big in California," he replied. "Not much more
than that; why?" he inquired.

"Well, I just got back from LA. Remember my friend Brian Kim?" I
asked.

"Yeah, you've talked about him before. Didn't he make a lot of money
in real estate?" he asked.

"He made a lot, and he lost a lot, I guess," I confided.

"Didn't know when to get out?" David surmised.

"Exactly. What goes up must come down. He kept buying when he
should have been selling," I answered.

"Happened to a lot of people," replied David.

"Yes, indeed. I got out just in time," I agreed.

"So what's he doing now?" David asked, seemingly interested.

"Growing marijuana," I replied.

I then began to recount everything I had seen and learned. I told him about the attorney I had met, Mark Kent, and how I could get a license for $3,500. I told him about Brian's grow house and the retail store in Venice Beach. David listened intently.

"How much can you make?" he asked with a flash of greed in his eye.

"Quite a bit," I assured him. "Pot costs about $600 per pound to grow and retails for eight times that amount."

"And it's legal?" he asked in disbelief.

"Yup, Prop 203 was a referendum by the people of California, and, according to Mark, only another referendum can overturn it. Neither judge, nor legislature…only the people can overturn it."

"So what is the opportunity?" He got to the point.

"Brian wants me to become partners and open up a retail space, while he builds a larger grow facility."

"Are you thinking about it?" he asked.

"I can't think about anything else, to be honest. Nothing else makes sense in this economy. I have to find something to make some money," I answered. "I'm coming to you for your opinion…and perhaps to even offer you a piece of the action if you can help finance the store."

"Interesting" was all he replied as he contemplated all I had just revealed.

"If you think this is a bad idea, I'm giving you veto power over my decisions," I told him. "If you say, 'No, don't do it,' I won't."

"Isn't it still against federal law?" David asked.

"Yes, but Obama is going to make an announcement once he takes office, stopping the raids. As they say, timing is everything," I encouraged.

He thought about it briefly, then a glow of excitement came across his face.

"Sounds exciting to me," he replied. "I say, 'Yes!'"

With that, I was faced with the stark reality that I was moving to LA. The pros outweighed the cons. Even my conservative friend thought it was a great opportunity. California, here I come…

I left the meeting with my mind made up, but the thought of LA made me cringe.

Brian called early Monday, which was 3:00 p.m. for him. He didn't beat around the bush; he asked about the loan.

"Sure," I said. "I just need to put together a note for you to sign."

"Have you thought about the opportunity?" he asked.

"Yeah, I still need to think about that," I informed him, not wanting to tip my hand just yet.

In business, I've found that the most emotional person always loses. Brian was eager and desperate. That gave me the upper hand. He needed money. I had money. I was in the driver's seat.

"When can I get the money?" he pressured.

"I'll deposit it in your account once I have the signed note. I'll type it up tonight," I promised.

"Can you do $10,000, instead of $5,000?" he asked, upping the whole deal in an instant.

"No," I replied. "I don't feel comfortable with that."

I just shook my head.

"What am I getting myself into?" I wondered. If I only knew half of what I know now, I would have hung up and changed my number.

That night, I put together the note and emailed it to Brian late that evening. There was the amount, the interest rate, the payoff date, and a signature line. At about 11:30 p.m., Brian called. It was way past my usual business hours.

"Are you really going to charge me $5,000 interest," he asked, "for only two months?" I listened in disbelief.

"Brian, this is *your* deal. I don't want to loan any money, honestly. You offered this return. If you don't want to do it, I'm fine with that," I stated, a little annoyed to say the least.

"No, it's fine," Brian answered.

He promised to FedEx me the note the next day, and it arrived the following morning. I followed Brian's instructions and deposited the money in his Chase account. He called me at 3:00 p.m. again, half awake.

"Got the money," he said. "When are you coming back to LA?"

"How about Monday?" I offered. "I've decided to take you up on the offer. Let's do this. I'm gonna draw up a partnership agreement, and we can discuss the details when I get there."

"All right," Brian exclaimed. "I'll set up a time to meet with Mark again while you are here."

"Sounds good. I'll email you my itinerary once I've booked it."

"OK," Brian said. "We are going to be rich," he promised.

"Or arrested," I said only half-jokingly as we hung up the phone.

Chapter 5: Moving Forward

The week went by quickly. I spent my time preparing the agreement. I kind of fancied myself an amateur attorney as I had written several partnership agreements before. I made sure to include a buy/sell agreement for the partners, as I fully realized that not all partnerships work out. Still, I felt confident Brian was a decent business person and that any conflict we had would be resolved easily. Sometimes money blinds us from the truth.

I then went to work on a projected budget. I needed to understand the numbers better before I could understand how much capital was going to be needed. I had $150,000 sitting in my checking account. I had over $200,000 in unused credit lines. I wrote down all the key operating statistics that I was aware of.

No matter what type of business you're in, most statistics are similar. Rent, employees, utilities, and the like. Advertising is always the biggest question mark and for me always a big number. The more you spend, the more you earn as long as you spend it wisely and effectively. Too many advertising options, especially online, are willing to take your money without providing results. My biggest question marks were revenues and cost of goods. These numbers I would need to get from Mark and Brian.

Now, I'm no computer expert, but I had become somewhat proficient in writing Excel spreadsheets for business. I was quite proud of my final product and saved it on my laptop. I played the numbers to see what kind of profit could be made. I tried to be conservative in my projections. I tried to start with my breakeven point and build from there.

Brian had told me the cost of goods was approximately 20 percent, so the profits looked great. I was getting more and more excited.

Once finished with that, I began brainstorming a name. Now, a good name leaves a clear mental picture. It touches the senses. I must have written down a hundred names, as I just let my ideas flow onto paper. On our next phone call, Brian told me he had another name and that he had been keeping it a secret. He would only tell me when our agreement was in place. I just hoped it was better than "The Bakery."

Monday came, and Brian met me at LAX. We got on the 405 and headed north.

"Where to?" I asked.

"We have to get you a state ID and a doctor's recommendation," Brian said.

"Can I get a state ID and have an AZ driver's license?" I asked.

"Yes, you have to have a state ID to get a recommendation and a license," he informed me.

"Lead the way," I said, putting my entire trust in my soon-to-be partner. We went to the license bureau, and I filled out the paperwork. I presented two forms of ID, and they told me I would receive my ID in six weeks. In the meantime, they issued a temporary.

"Six weeks?" I thought in disgust. In Arizona, I would be walking out with ID in hand on the same visit. "What a backward state," I thought.

"Don't worry," Brian said. "It's good enough for our purposes."

We jumped back on the highway, hitting lunch traffic...although who am I kidding? The traffic is always this bad. Don't blame lunch. People on the road were rude and drove erratically. I tried to put this nuisance out of my mind.

We arrived in a downtown area, with tall buildings. I was still very new to LA and couldn't tell you where I was or where I had been. The city just looked like it all ran together, strangled by traffic jams.

We found the buildings we were looking for and then began looking for parking…a usual theme in LA. Brian seemed to know what he was doing, marching through the steps necessary to get the job done. It would have taken me months to figure all this out. Brian had been in LA for two years, so he definitely had the advantage. I felt like a fish out of water, so I followed obediently.

The doctor's office was on the seventh floor of a high rise. We went to the elevator and hit the up button. The elevator opened immediately and took us to the desired floor. Inside the doctor's office, there were about twelve people ahead of me. As we walked in, I scanned the group of patients. Most fit your typical profile of someone who would smoke marijuana, but there were a couple that stood out. One man was dressed in a business suit, and there was a little old lady with a streak of pink in her hair. Brian went right to the counter and announced we were there. An attractive young lady with dark curly black hair and dork-rimmed glasses motioned to us to sign in and fill out some paperwork. She gave Brian a clipboard with the typical questionnaire you receive when you visit the doctor. She looked at me and asked if I needed one also, but I told her no. This one was for me.

Brian and I proceeded to take a seat, and I began filling out the paperwork with medical history, allergies, etc. Brian began to coach me on what to write down.

"Tell them you have chronic pain in your lower back. They can't prove or disprove that," he said.

So that's exactly what I did.

Once completed, I took it back to the young lady and turned it in. She gave me a sweet smile and said the doctor would review it and call me when ready. As she reached to place it into the basket, I noticed a small black heart tattoo placed strategically on her inner breast right near the bra line. Her nails were also painted black, so I was beginning to notice a theme. I wondered what other treasures were hidden under those clothes.

"I'm starting to like LA," I thought.

After about fifteen minutes of waiting, another young lady emerged from behind a closed door and called my name. This lady was about five foot, two, I would guess, and a little on the chubby side. She was dressed in a blue uniform, sort of like what a nurse would wear. We walked to a small room on the side of the hallway, and she motioned for me to enter. There was a scale and measuring stick, and she took my height and weight. She then asked me to sit down as she wrapped a blood pressure apparatus around my left arm.

I knew the drill, so I uncrossed my legs and just relaxed.

"Wow, 180 over 90," she said. "It's a little high. Is that normal for you?"

"Pretty much," I replied. "Been that way since my twenties."

"Are you taking medication for it?" she asked

"Yes, lisinopril and aspirin," I responded, "but I'm out and need to get my prescription refilled."

"We can probably get that done for you also while you are here," she stated.

"That would be awesome," I replied.

"OK, come with me," she said as she removed the blood pressure wrap.

We walked further down the hall to a larger room with an examination table in it.

"Have a seat and the doctor will be with you shortly," she promised. With that, she left the room, closing the door behind her.

I began checking my text messages as I waited. Ten minutes went by, then twenty, then thirty. These things always take longer than you think. About forty-five minutes into it, the door opened and a small, petite, dark-skinned man walked in.

"I am Doctor Patel," he announced with a thick Indian accent. "How are you doing today?"

"I'm good, doctor," I replied.

"You say you have back problems? Can you show me where?" he inquired.

"Right here," I said as I pointed to my lower back.

"I see," he said. "Can you stand up for me?"

"Yes," I replied, continuing with the charade. I slid off the table and stood facing the doctor.

"Bend forward as if you were going to touch your toes but stop when the pain begins," he instructed.

I bent to about a forty-five-degree angle, then stopped. "OK now," I said dishonestly. I felt dumb having to lie about this, but I think both of us knew what was happening. This was a factory for doctors' recommendations, nothing more. He didn't care about my pain and I didn't have any. We were going through the motions.

"On a scale from one to ten, how bad is your pain?" he asked.

"About a seven or eight," I replied, thinking that was a good number.

"OK, have a seat," he instructed. I will send Wendy back for you when we are ready. With that, he left the office. Five minutes later, the little,

chubby girl returned (presumably Wendy), and she had a pink recommendation card in hand.

"You're all set," she said. "Just go out to the front counter and pay. I'll
come with you."

We went back to the window together, I paid my $160, and they
handed me my recommendation. It was as simple as that. Brian jumped
up from the seat, and we both made our way down the elevator.

"Pretty simple, huh?" he said.

"Yeah, not bad," I said, still surprised by the ease of it all. Yup, as I suspected, Californians had just figured out a way to get high legally.

We got down to the first level and made our way out into the parking
lot. Brian pushed his keypad and his SUV beeped, drawing us toward it.
It was a little overcast, which surprised me because you always hear about
sunny California.

Once in the car, I asked Brian what was next, and he told me we had
to go pay Mark and get that in motion. We proceeded out of the parking
lot and back onto the highway. Forty-five minutes later, we arrived in Van
Nuys again. We went to the same coffee shop as we had been to before,
and as we walked in, I saw Mark's now familiar face and grin. He seemed
like a kind and knowledgeable person, but I'm sure he was most excited
about getting paid.

"You're back," he said. "I knew you would be. I saw the light bulb go
off in your head the last time you were here. Ready to start making some
money?" he asked.

"Yeah, let's do this," I said as I extended my hand and sat down at
the table. Butch raised his head from behind Mark's leg but didn't bother
getting up this time. Brian grabbed a seat beside me, and you could tell he
was giddy that his dream was coming together.

"I've put together a simple agreement for you to read and review and then sign. First of all, know that I am not acting as an attorney. I always advise people to retain their own legal counsel, but that's just a formality."

As I read through the agreement, it stated just that. It stated that I was to pay a flat fee of $3,500 and, at the end, I would have a *hardship exemption* filed with the city. That this hardship was not to be confused with a license but was good enough to begin operations. I signed the agreement and pulled out my checkbook. Once I've made a decision, I move forward without further apprehension; $3,500 seemed like a steal for all this experience at one table.

"Now remember, the next step is to find a location," he said. "I can help you with talking to the landlord if they have any apprehensions, which some of them will indeed. Do you know in what area you would like to locate your store?" he asked.

"We want to be on the west side, near Santa Monica and Venice Beach," Brian chimed in.

"Good area," Mark agreed. "Go to Weed Tracker, which is a website where you can locate the current store locations and find an area that is underserviced," he suggested. "I suggest you then canvass that area looking for 'for rent' signs and contact the owners. Don't tell them immediately what you are looking for; just tell them you need a retail space. You should meet each person face to face before you tell them your real mission. Earn their trust and get them excited about some new renters. Build some rapport."

"Got it. No problem," I agreed. You see, for many years, I was a cold call salesperson who went business to business, so I was used to rejection. I didn't believe finding a building would be a problem. Mark pulled up a map of the west side and suggested some areas in which to begin our search.

"Tell me when you've got a fish on the line, and let me know if you need my help reeling it in," he smiled. "I'm excited for you guys; you're gonna do great."

With that, we shook hands, and Brian and I left the coffee shop.

"Take me to the area he was talking about, and I'll find a hotel close by so we can really begin our search," I said. By now, it was already 1:00 p.m., and we were about an hour north of our target area. Brian first took me to Santa Monica and showed me the pier area. I told him to stop because I wanted to walk out on the boardwalk, but he said he didn't have time.

Brian was all business all the time. He never took the time to smell the roses. I saw a large Holiday Inn just blocks from the pier, so I pulled out my telephone and went to my hotel app. I was in town for three days this time, so I might as well stay somewhere fun, right? The rooms were available for $150 per night, which I thought was a smoking deal, so I booked them immediately.

From Santa Monica, Brian then drove south to the Venice Beach area. Talk about night and day. Santa Monica was very clean and corporate-looking, but Venice Beach was a little dirtier, with many transients walking around. Traffic was thick, and it was hard to get close to the beach.

Brian informed me he needed to go back to the grow shop and asked if I wanted to come with him. "Hmmm," I thought. Hang out with Brian, a total stick in the mud, or go back to my room near Santa Monica pier. Not even a tough choice. I laughed to myself.

"No, take me to my room," I instructed. "I want to get on some computers and begin searching for a location."

Brian turned the car back toward Santa Monica, which took about twenty minutes to arrive at the hotel.

"I may rent a car tomorrow, so that you can take care of what you need to do, and I can do what I need to do," I informed Brian.

"OK, sounds good. I'll be available at about 3:00 p.m. tomorrow. I still have to drive a cab to pay the bills until we get this going," he said.

"No worries," I assured him. Honestly, I really didn't need his help with this next step. He would be more of a hindrance with his lack of people skills.

"Oh, by the way, do you mind if I grab a bud for tonight from the back? I still have to do my research, you know," I said, laughingly.

"Yeah, no problem," Brian said, looking a little annoyed. You see if it didn't benefit Brian, he wasn't interested. This is what I came to learn over the next few months.

So with that, I exited the SUV and made my way into the hotel lobby. I was a little surprised at how dated the lobby seemed. Old carpet, old furniture. It definitely needed some updating. That's probably why it had a good price. At the front desk was a young Black gentleman, dressed in a sharp-looking vest and a tie. He had underneath a nicely pressed white shirt with long sleeves. His name tag said Daryl.

"Welcome to the Holiday Inn, Santa Monica. Do you have a reservation?" he asked.

"I do, indeed," I replied and proceeded to give him my name and credit card info. Once I received my keys, I made my way to the seventh floor. Daryl had been nice enough to give me a room facing the ocean as he realized this was my first time in Santa Monica and that I was excited. Still, I couldn't help but notice I seemed to be the only one in the hotel other than Daryl.

I went to my room, and it was very unimpressive with the same out-dated decor and popcorn ceilings.

"Yup, definitely could use some updating," I said to myself again. I searched for the suitcase holder, that little wooden thing that folds out to hold your case, and opened it up. I plopped my suitcase down on it and popped it open. I was a man on a mission. This time, I didn't forget the rolling papers. Time for a little R and R. I crushed the bud on a small tray on the desk, then rolled myself up a good-sized joint.

I then walked onto the balcony and lit that baby up. "The Original Gangster," I said to myself. "Not bad."

Within minutes, my body began to float. A smile spread across my face, and all my worries left me. Here I was, sitting on a balcony, overlooking an ocean. The breeze was caressing my face as the sun was moving ever so slowly toward the horizon.

"Life is good," I thought. "Nothing but adventures lie ahead."

I felt very lucky to be here in the present moment. Alone with my thoughts and my dreams. I walked in to lie down on the bed for a while and to just enjoy being alive. I drifted off into a deep sleep—one filled with joy and wonder. I dreamt about beaches and beautiful women. Now, when you dream when you are high, the dreams are always more intense and more real. Sometimes you even realize you are dreaming, so you gain total control of the dream. That's when the real fun begins. Those beautiful women on the beaches become a lot more accommodating once you gain control of the dream.

A couple of hours later, I woke up horny and alone. Still feeling the effects of the OG, I made my way to the balcony. The sun was just getting ready to set, and I saw that the pier had come alive with action. Lights and sounds blared, and the large Ferris wheel had begun to operate. In my relaxed and curious state of mind, I decided to go check this out for myself. But before that…perhaps another puff was in order. I hit the pipe again, then grabbed my room key, wallet, and phone and headed out the door, down the elevator, and to the lobby. Another person was working and didn't even look up as I exited the hotel.

Getting my bearings, I determined the pier must be somewhat to my south and then directly west. Things always seem much closer until you start walking to them. It took about a half hour to get there, and I decided on the way back that I would take a cab.

Walking onto the boardwalk was like walking back in time in a way. I felt like I was entering an old-fashioned carnival. There were games and prizes and ice cream stands and cotton candy. I first stopped by an arcade that was filled with pinball machines and other games from days gone by. To the right, I saw a Bubba Gump restaurant, which looked inviting as I had worked up a thirst on my walk, not to mention the dry mouth that occurs with it. Beyond that, to my left, was the large Ferris wheel, which had a small line.

I walked into the Bubba Gump restaurant, where I was greeted by three beautiful hostesses. I told them I was looking for the bar, and they pointed me in the right direction. The bar was hustling and bustling pretty well for a Monday night. The bartender, a red-haired man in his early thirties, was friendly and efficient. I felt like I was truly immersing myself in my new-found home. A few Jack-and-Cokes later, I decided to make my way back to the hotel.

As planned, I grabbed a taxi for a very short drive. Still, with tip, it was fifteen dollars, but it was well worth it in my condition. I don't remember going through the lobby or if anyone was at the counter, but I made it up to my room quickly. Once inside, I grabbed what was left of my joint and hit the patio again.

"Third time's the charm," I thought and drew a deep drag. That one hit me pretty solid, so I made my way to the room and had a short coughing spasm. Luckily there was complimentary water left by the hotel so I wolfed half of that down, which calmed my cough. My eyes were watering profusely, but I felt absolutely amazing.

I turned on the TV and started listening to music. I was in a total state of euphoria. What could be better than this? I thought. But then it came to me. I knew what would make this even better… some company.

"Why not? I'm living the dream, right?"

So I opened up my computer and started to search the classifieds. No surprise, in Los Angeles, there were many ladies looking to provide company. The key was to be able to filter through the bullshit and find a genuine opportunity. A real girl with real service. I believe I had perfected that to an art.

Of course, the first thing everyone always looks at is the photos. Of course, those can be very misleading so you must always confirm they are real. If they lie to you, then you have every right to call them out at the door and refuse service. Next, you must pin them down on price and service. There are many games being played online, so I've learned you must be direct and to the point and say, "Is the price flat rate and full service?" If they say anything other than yes, the conversation is over.

So as I perused the ads, I decided I was in the mood for an Asian girl. Asian girls were always a good choice—usually not too many games. What you see is what you get. Usually, they work with a service, and they want repeat customers. Well, I dialed the phone, an Asian woman answered, and I asked her the screening questions. When I asked about the photos, she said, "Don't worry. I will send you a beautiful girl, don't worry," so I said, "OK."

When I asked about the price, she said, "Don't worry. Just one price; don't worry." I wasn't worried. I gave her my hotel and room number, and we made an appointment.

About an hour later, my phone rang and the same lady was on the phone. She said, "The girl is at your room door. Please open up."

When I opened it, I was very pleasantly surprised to see a beautiful young Japanese girl standing there. She gave me a little bow as she walked into my room and took my hand to lead me toward the bed.

She asked me to touch her to prove I wasn't a cop, and then she touched me in a similar manner.

She said, "You pay first" as she pointed to the dresser.

I laid the money down and sat down on the bed. She counted the money and set it back on the dresser. She then proceeded to pull her short dress over her head, revealing a red thong and bra. She walked to the bathroom and grabbed a towel, which she laid on the bed. She began removing my clothes, which I eagerly complied with. She then went down on her knees and put me inside her mouth. Wow. By this time, I was hard as a rock. This was definitely not her first time.

She then told me to get on the bed and as I did, she pulled out a condom and removed her panties and bra. She climbed on top of me as she put some lubricant inside of her. Then she began to work herself onto me as her eyes opened wide.

"You big boy," she said as her pussy enveloped me. She began to slide her slim body up and down. Her breasts were small but perky, and I buried my head into them. She then changed positions so she was facing away from me. Her perfect body was riding me like a dream.

She then turned and asked, "You top now?"

She was obviously tired from her efforts. I think she thought she would have finished me by now, but, honestly, I was just getting started.

"You want doggy?" she asked as she slid forward on the bed.

"How can I say no to that?" I responded as I entered her from behind. I pinned her down from behind and began kissing the back of her neck, which she obviously liked. I breathed in her ear to really get her going.

Her body started to convulse, and I could tell that she was coming. I decide to hold off, so I could see her from the front side. I could tell that since she had come, she was now ultra-sensitive, so when I rolled her over, she was gonna really enjoy it. Up until now, I had been slow and purposeful. Now I was going to give it to her hard. As I entered her, I began pounding her so hard against the bed that we both bounced up about three inches with each thrust. Sweat started to stream down my forehead and chest as I ravaged this girl's sexy body. I whispered to her, "Do you want me to come?" and she said, "Yes, please come; please come."

With that, I exploded inside her. My legs were shaking as I fell back beside her. I was exhausted.

She said, "Wow, you really fucked me. It's been a long time."

I laughed. "Yeah, that was good, huh," I agreed.

"Yes, very good," she said.

We both lay there exhausted until she gathered the strength to start moving.

"I must go; it's very late," she said. With that, she texted someone on her phone, got dressed, and headed for the door. We hugged and she left.

I hit the bed still exhausted from the experience.

The next morning, I awoke at about 5:30 a.m., which was kind of normal for me. The sun was not up yet as I looked out at the balcony. I went back to the bathroom and started brewing a single-serve coffee cup. I really liked these because then coffee never went to waste and, more importantly, I didn't overdrink it and get jittery.

"Time to get serious," I thought. I set up my laptop and began searching the classifieds online. I identified about seven different locations over the next hour that looked like possibilities. At about 6:00 a.m., the sun started to rise, so I decided to go for a jog and burn off any leftover lag from the whiskey and weed. I ran down by the pier and south down the beach. Traffic was already heavy. After an hour, I returned to my room and took a shower. My goal was to be ready by 9:00 a.m. to start driving to look for properties.

First, I had to locate a rental car company near me. I chose Enterprise because they offered to pick me up at my hotel. By the time I got through all the paperwork, it was getting close to nine, so I drove my new rental back to the hotel and grabbed my list of locations.

The first location I saw was located just west of my hotel on Pico Boulevard. It seemed like an older, more established neighborhood.

"The key to picking out a good location," Mark had told me, "is to have good visibility, good traffic, good parking, and not be in a five-star neighborhood."

Like Mark had warned, if the people living in the neighborhood don't like the fact that you are there, it will cause you a lot of problems in the future. The storefront was small and it was located right next to a *llantera*, which is Spanish for a tire shop. Across the street, there was a neighborhood bar called the Joker and next to that was an Asian massage parlor. This was exactly the "seedy" type of neighborhood that would not attract too much attention. The main problem I saw was very little parking. As I drove around behind the storefront, it looked like approximately six spaces were dedicated to this shop and the area was run down, with a large dumpster as a decoration. I could only imagine what it looked like at night. It just didn't seem safe.

I didn't bother to call the property manager to view this locale for those reasons and went on to the next property. This property was located in a little-known suburb called Mar Vista. It was located near the intersection of Centinela and Venice Boulevard. It was only about five miles away from my current location, so I arrived there pretty quickly. When I pulled up in front, I was pleasantly surprised by the metered parking spots, of which there were about fifteen. Right next to the store was what appeared to be an "urban" clothing store and next to that was a Chinese restaurant. Immediately to the left, the building looked vacant, and after that was your typical neighborhood liquor store. The storefront showed well, so I decided to drive around to the back alley and see what that was like. Like any back alley in a big city, it was a little dingy, but I drove to the back side of the store to have a look. At the back, there was a large chain link fence, which had to be at least ten feet high. There was a sturdy chain securing the gate and about a twenty-foot trailer parked inside. When I say trailer, I mean a modular unit, similar to what someone would live in.

"Interesting," I thought. Besides the trailer, there were a few tires and room for about two vehicles to park. When I got out of the vehicle, I just had this overwhelming sensation or feeling come over me that this exact spot is where I would die. I've never had the feeling before or since.

I got back in my car quickly and drove back to the front of the building. Being a Tuesday, traffic was pretty heavy, and Venice Boulevard was a major thoroughfare. Of the fifteen metered parking spots, only about five were in use, which made me think that the parking would be adequate. I parked at a meter and dropped a quarter in, which gave me fifteen minutes to explore. I walked over to the large glass windows and peered inside the unit. It was a large open space with a balcony area constructed over the back half. It had cement floors and block walls—totally open for whatever design we wanted to implement.

I thought to myself, "Well, this one is at least worth a conversation."

So I called the number posted on the building.

"Can I help you?" a female voice answered with a medium East coast accent.

"Yes, I'm outside of a retail building located on Venice Blvd in Mar Vista."

"Sure; what can I tell you about it?" the voice responded.

"Well, what are the square footage, zoning, and your lease terms, to start?" I responded.

"Sure," she said in a definite New York accent. Probably Brooklyn by the way she dragged out the "u" in "sure."

"Well, it is a little over 6,000 square feet. The rent is $6,500 per month, and we are looking for a minimum of a three-year term," she responded.

"Is that a triple net lease or is that a flat lease?" I inquired.

"No, it's flat," she responded. "Of course, you pay for your own utilities and such."

"Do you offer any build-out incentives?" I asked, "Because it will take some time to get this unit functional for our purposes."

"It's all negotiable," she said. "What did you have in mind?"

"Well, I'm pretty straightforward, so I was thinking three months free for our build-out and a three-year contract," I suggested.

"Yeah, that wouldn't be a problem," she confirmed. This was actually a pretty standard deal.

"Are you working with a broker?" she asked, wondering if she would be paying commissions to anyone.

"Nope, it's just me," I replied.

"Well, that's a bonus," she replied.

"When can we set up a view of the location?" I inquired. "My name is Dalton, by the way."

"My name is Lisbeth," she answered in kind. "Well, I'm the owner and live close by so I could show it to you in a few hours. I'm just finishing some things up. Or I could show you tomorrow. You tell me what's good," she suggested.

"Let's shoot for tomorrow," I suggested. "I would want to have some of my partners with me to get their input," I explained.

"OK, tomorrow I'm available after 3:00 p.m.," Lisbeth offered.

"Three should be perfect," I said but I was concerned, remembering this was Brian's wake-up hour. "Take down my name and number and I will see you at three tomorrow," I told her.

We exchanged info and that was that. I was very excited about this location, but we still had to overcome a major obstacle. She had never asked about our intended use. How would she react when she realized what our product was? This is why I wanted to have Mark with me to explain all the legalities of it once we had built some rapport.

Immediately, I got on the phone with Mark and told him about our three o'clock appointment. He assured me he would be there and was very excited about the location. Next, I called Brian. Of course, there was no answer as it was 11:30, and he was probably in la-la land about now. Especially if he had eaten an edible.

I had one more location to look at. This one was located in Culver City, a few miles to the west. As reached the city limits, I could tell a definite change in the feel of the area. It was much better kept, and there was a large presence of police. I drove by the storefront but honestly, it seemed way too upscale, with clothing shops and nice restaurants. I opted not to do further research on this one. My fingers were crossed on the Mar Vista location. I seemed to have had a good rapport started with Lizbeth.

With that, I decided to explore some more. I had heard a lot about Venice Beach and wanted to go down and have some lunch and get a feel for my new-found home. I'm kind of a history buff and I had heard Jim Morrison had a house down on Venice Beach so I thought it was worth a look.

My MapQuest told me that it was located on Westminster Speedway, so I followed the instructions to get there. On the way there, I shot straight down Venice Blvd again and passed the earlier location. A few miles more and I noticed I was passing Lincoln Blvd very close to The Farmacy, which I had visited with Brian. I had a little flower with me so didn't think I needed to stop. I did start to get a feel for my general location, however, which made me feel more secure in my decision to relocate to LA.

Once I reached Westminster road, I needed to turn left or right. I chose right because I saw a public parking sign that accepted credit cards. As luck would have it, my battery on my phone had just died so now I was pretty much on my own to explore the old-fashioned way by just walking. I wanted to find a beach bar that perhaps had an electric outlet where I could recharge.

I located one right on the beach just a few blocks from my intended destination but decided recharging was my first priority as I was still waiting for Brian's confirmation phone call. The bar had an outdoor patio that faced the beach, but I went inside and sat close to the bartender to see if I could build enough rapport to get a "charge out of him." I laughed at my own joke. The bartender was a friendly female with a kind face and a great smile. She asked me what I wanted and I told her my usual reply of a Jack-and-Coke. She asked if I wanted to look at the menu, which I did, and I ordered some chicken nachos.

"Oh no," I said to her in fake disbelief. "I'm supposed to meet a friend down here, and my phone just died. I was just going to text him my location. You don't have an outlet I could borrow, do you?" I inquired.

"Sure, if you have a charger, I can hook you up," she replied.

"I do have that," I replied as I pulled the charger out of my pocket and handed it to her. She took my phone and my charger and plugged them into an outlet right on the center island in full view but out of reach. I was hoping there was an outlet close by where I could still use my phone, but beggars can't be choosers, right? That's what I get for drinking, smoking, and partying with wild women until all hours of the night, I prodded myself.

"Oh well, worth it," I thought as the foggy memories of the little Japanese girl filled my mind and my body.

I wolfed down the nachos and then asked to view my phone. It had about a 50 percent charge, which was good enough for me. I faked a call to my imaginary friend and explained to the bartender that they weren't going to make it after all. I paid my bill and walked out to explore. The beach was wide and open, so I thought, in the tradition of Jim Morrison, it would be better to view his house for the first time "high." I walked out into the sand until I was quite alone. There I took a couple of hits on my joint that I had rolled this morning and again the feeling of euphoria hit me. With a deep relaxing breath, I set out on my new adventure. A few blocks down, I found the Jim Morrison apartments. They were an antique green color and had balconies on the second level. There was not really much to see there quite honestly, but then I noticed an unusual building next door, which caught my eye.

Atop the building, there were larger-than-life statues of what appeared to be Greek and Roman gods, as well as gargoyles and other mystical creatures. Upon closer inspection, this house was purported to be haunted and was available for tours. I wasn't up for a tour but sure enjoyed my time just looking at each of the statues. I decide to take a stroll down the beach and see what else Venice Beach had to offer. As I walked down the boardwalk, it was lined with tattoo parlors, tie-dye shirt shops, and smoke shops. There were jewelry carts on the walkway, and everyone was trying to get you to come and look in their stores.

A hot blonde whizzed by me on Rollerblades, and I got to enjoy the view of her backside as she pulled away. Her little shorts had the word Pink on them...

"Why do they have to tease like that?" I chuckled. Her perfect body was spoiled by a large tattoo, which covered the majority of her back. "Why would you mess with God's perfection?" I asked myself.

The beach turned into a grassy area with palm trees and pathways that went closer to the ocean, which was still a good distance away. I decided to go right to the water so I began up one of the pathways. Throughout this parklike setting, there were homeless people hunkered down under plastic tarps as if planning to spend the night there.

As I looked at my phone, I saw that it was 3:05 p.m., and, of course, like clockwork, Brian's name appeared on the caller ID as my phone started to vibrate and ring.

"He must be awake," I realized.

Hello," I said.

"Dalton, it's Brian," was the response on the other end.

"No shit," I thought.

"So you found a spot?" he inquired, obviously half-asleep.

"Possibly," I said. "We have a meeting tomorrow. At 3:00 p.m."

"OK, sounds good. Send me the address, and I'll see you then," he promised.

"Sounds good," I agreed. I was more than happy to keep this short and sweet as I was enjoying my buzz and Brian was quite a buzz kill. With that, Brian hung up the phone and I could go back to my Venice Beach adventure. As I drew nearer to the ocean, I could see a large concrete structure blocking my path. It seemed to have a lot of people around it and inside I kept seeing people's heads popping up and down. As I got very close, I saw that these bobbing heads were actually skateboarders and this was a very well-thought-out skate park. I watched in amazement as these young people, both male and female, displayed their incredible skills. You could tell it was a very competitive environment and that there was a hierarchy among the skaters themselves.

"I don't know how they do it, man," I thought to myself.

I remember the first time I tried to jump my bicycle over a ramp that my friend had constructed when I was eight. I hit the gravel and pavement and was pulling gravel out of my hands for weeks. That was the end of my daredevil career right then and there, I decided.

I walked further down the boardwalk and found myself in front of Muscle Beach. I guess this is where Arnold Schwarzenegger did his work-outs long before he was famous. It was 6:00 p.m. by now, and I thought it was high time to be heading back. The sun was getting low on the horizon, which was normal for late December. I noticed that the boardwalk was much less busy at this time and was beginning to get a bit sketchy. As I walked, a couple of young Black men approached me and asked if I could help them out by supporting their music. They stuck an earbud up to my ear, and I could hear a rapper going on about killing cops or something.

Now I'm not really a rap fan, but I thought what the heck, so I bought one of their CDs for ten bucks. They offered two for fifteen, but I declined. It was pretty dark by the time I got back to my car, and it seemed the only ones still out were the homeless and the con artists, looking for unsuspecting tourists. Venice Beach was definitely not a night spot. Note to self.

As I started my car, I realized I was still quite buzzed and didn't really know how to get back to the hotel. I put it in MapQuest again, and it appeared to be a straight shot down the Pacific highway. I drove extra carefully as I wasn't used to driving in such a condition. This is when paranoia sets in, and I can tell you the drive back was not fun. Note to self: Only smoke at your final destination or take a cab. Uber hadn't arrived on the scene quite yet.

Once back at the hotel, I took a long shower, lay on the bed, and fell asleep quickly. I awoke at about 3:00 a.m., wide awake as usual. I'm a morning person, which sometimes can be a curse. I decided to spend the morning looking up other locations in case this one didn't work out. I gave this one a fifty-fifty chance. At about six, I went down for a continental breakfast and coffee.

"No pot smoking today," I decided. There was too much to get done. I needed to be alert. I spent the rest of the morning on my balcony just researching everything I could about the area.

The day dragged until two o'clock arrived, and I got ready to leave. I hit the road and was at the location in less than twenty minutes, so I was incredibly early. Yes, I'm one of those people who are always early to every appointment, usually way early. This drives me crazy because a lot of others are perpetually late, which makes my wait time even longer. Oh well. It gave me more time to check out the area. I decided to check out some other local dispensaries in the area to check out the competition. My Weed Tracker map found one with high ratings a few blocks south on Washington Boulevard. I drove over to that one and pulled into the parking lot. There were only a few cars in the lot, so I got out and went inside. As I entered, I was greeted by the security guard who asked to see my recommendation and my ID. He also wanded me, and I pulled out my keys to show him what was in my pockets. He then opened the door to the dispensary, and I entered the main room. Inside, there were glass counters very similar to The Farmacy. A male and female employee both welcomed me, and the female invited me to come to her register.

"Are you new or returning?" she asked.

"It's my first time here," I responded.

"That's awesome," she replied. "I just need to get your recommendation and ID and I'll get you all set up."

I gave her what she asked for, and she proceeded to enter the information into her computer. Once complete, she asked me to step in front of a camera and proceeded to take my photo. It was obvious she had done this many times before. My photo was printed from a nearby printer, and she then encased it in plastic and handed me my new "membership" card.

"You are now official," she announced. "What can I get for you?"

"Damn, I wish the DMV was this efficient," I exclaimed, incredibly happy with the service.

"I know, right?" she said, as she awaited my selections.

Now they had all types of different strains listed on the board as well as a case full of edibles. Since I still had some weed back in the room, I thought I might give edibles a try. She showed me a variety of cookies, drinks, hard candies, and even lollipops, but when she pulled out the gummy bears, she had me hook, line, and sinker.

"I've got to try those for sure," I said. "And give me a brownie also," I added.

"Is that all for today?" she asked.

"That should do it," I confirmed. With that, she rang up my order and I attempted to pay by debit card.

"I'm sorry, but we can only accept cash," she said. She informed me it was a federal law. "Luckily, we have an ATM right over there."

The order was only $26, so I reached into my wallet and pulled out $40. As I received my change, I looked at my clock and realized I only had seven minutes to get to my appointment to view the space.

"Dang it, I hate to be late," I thought.

I jumped in the car and made my way back to Venice Boulevard. I made it with two minutes to spare. The front door of the space was propped open and someone was inside, so I parked, paid the meter, and made my way to the door. As I entered, I noticed a short woman in the back facing away from me.

"Hello," I announced, not wanting to scare her. She turned and smiled and began to walk toward me. She appeared to be in her midfifties, but I was excited to see a large purple strand of hair projecting from her otherwise normal-looking hairdo. I was hoping for an old hippie.

"You must be Lizbeth?" I inquired.

"Yes, and you're Dalton?" she asked.

"Yes indeed. Have my partners shown up yet?" I inquired.

"Not yet," she stated. Just then, Mark appeared in the doorway.

"Let me introduce you to Mark. He is a retired attorney and now a business consultant helping me navigate Los Angeles, as I'm from Arizona," I explained.

"How do you do?" Mark offered a handshake, and Lizbeth accepted.

"We are just waiting for Brian," I said as the minutes ticked away. "Do you mind if I explore while we are waiting?" I asked.

"No, go right ahead," she waved me inward.

"Now, I'm really curious about this loft area. What was it used for?" I asked.

"Well, it was a retail store, and they used it to display items of clothing. They just recently closed up shop and are still on the hook for another year of the lease unless someone else comes in," she explained.

"I noticed a modular home in the back. What's that all about?" I asked.

"Oh, the last tenant still needs to move that," she replied.

"Oh, OK" is all I could say. I inspected the loft, which was nothing more than a large open area, and then went to the back around the stairway. The stairway was just unfinished wood. The floor was just white concrete. Not much decorating had gone into the last shop. A small bathroom was in the back section and then some double steel doors exited out the back. I popped the doors open to again see the chain link fences and the modular trailer. I walked outside to get a better look and popped open the trailer. It had obviously been used for storage and was not weathertight. A musky smell came from the carpet, and there appeared to be one bedroom. The bathroom was disgusting and hadn't been used in a while.

"Thank God." Lizbeth reminded me that that would be moved.

"Thirty-five minutes have gone by and still no sign of Brian," I stated. Mark rolled his eyes but kept silent.

"I think this might be a regular occurrence," I thought.

"So what type of business do you have?" Lizbeth said, finally asking the million-dollar question. I looked at Mark, and he looked at me.

I jumped right in. "Well, we have a retail shop," I said trying to gloss over the question for a moment. "Do you have time for a cup of coffee so we can go over things in more detail?" I asked.

"Sure," she concurred. "We can just walk across the street," she offered. With that, she locked up the shop, and we made our way to the crosswalks.

"Seems like a lot of drive-by traffic," I said, just trying to make conversation.

"Yeah, this road is always busy," she agreed.

Once we got to the shop, we placed our order, and then we got down to business.

"So I wanted you to be sitting down when we discussed this because I didn't know how you would feel about the subject," I led in. "How do you feel about medical marijuana?"

"I'm all for it," she said. "In fact, I even have a recommendation myself." She smiled.

A great feeling of relief filled my body. "Awesome, then maybe this won't be a hard sell," I joked. "You see, Mark is an expert in the field and is helping me get set up with my licensing and such, and we are looking for the perfect location…I think your location would be great."

"Wow, I had never thought about that, but I guess you are right," she said. "I guess my only concern is, aren't they still raiding stores? I wouldn't want that kind of attention on my property as I have other tenants."

"I understand that," I agreed. "But with the election of Barack Obama, he has already said he will be ending the raids, so by the time we get open, we should be fine."

Mark went into some detail about the law and where it was trending, and Lizbeth just sat and absorbed it all.

"Well, I don't have an issue with it, but let me talk to my husband and see what he says," she said.

"Do you think we should be with you to help explain?" I offered.

She laughed. "Don't worry, my husband is an old hippie. I'm the skeptical one. I'm sure he won't object."

I laughed as well. It sounded like it was a done deal.

"How soon would you want to move forward?" she asked.

"Well, I'm here until Friday, so I'd like to get everything finalized before then so I can return to Arizona and start packing up my house."

"We should be able to get that down," she said. "Let's meet tomorrow afternoon."

Just then, the phone rang. It was 4:00 p.m., and it was Brian.

"Sorry man, overslept again. I'm headed right down," he promised.

"No need," I said. "Mark and I handled everything."

"Can't you get her to wait?" he asked, feeling as if he was being left out.

"No, Brian. It's handled. She's gonna talk to her husband tonight, and if he approves, we are going to move forward. Here, talk to Mark." I handed him the phone as I walked Lizbeth to the door.

"See you tomorrow; I'm excited," I said.

"Me too," she agreed. With that, she left.

I came back to Mark, who was still on the phone with Brian. He handed me back the phone.

"I can't believe she couldn't wait," he said. "I could be there in half an hour."

"Brian, our meeting was at 3:00, not 4:30. One of my pet peeves is being late to a meeting, especially one this important," I scolded him.

"Well, what if I don't like it?" he asked.

"Well, Brian, you're gonna have to like it because I'm the one who is paying for everything. Don't worry; you'll like it. There's even a loft. I think we can build an apartment up there and save on rent. We might be meeting tomorrow around the same time. I'll let you know."

"OK," he said. Then we hung up.

"Great job, Dalton," Mark said with a grin. "You handled that perfectly. It's not that easy to find such a willing landlord."

"I know, we got lucky on that one," I agreed. "I hope hubby doesn't mess it up."

Mark agreed.

"Call me if you need me tomorrow. I'm free all day."

"You got it, Mark."

We shook hands, and Mark headed to his car. I felt great! This was all coming together as planned and ahead of schedule.

I got back to my hotel room and received notification of an email received. When I opened it, it was a rental application and credit check, which was pretty standard. She also had sent a copy of the lease for my review and informed me that her husband had no problem with our intended use.

I forwarded a copy of the lease to Mark and Brian and proceeded to fill out the application. Lizbeth offered to meet the next day at the same time and place, so I accepted. Things were looking good. I decided to smoke a bowl and get some sleep.

"Oh…that's now three days in a row. Hope I'm not becoming a stoner," I laughed to myself.

You see, I have an obsessive compulsiveness about things. If there is pizza in the fridge, I will eat the whole thing over a short period. If there is a bottle of whiskey in the house, I will drink the whole thing in a day, and if I have weed, I will smoke it consistently until it's gone. This is why I never keep alcohol or marijuana in my house. If I want some, I force myself to go get it and then only in a quantity that suits my purpose for right now. Then I'll go weeks and weeks without that vice—sometimes months. I also have a very strong tolerance to alcohol, which sucks because it takes large quantities to make me feel anything but normal. I contribute that to an overactive mind. Most people I know, such as my brother, sister, or son, have two drinks and are two sheets to the wind. I've pulled each of them out of drunken situations before even though I had probably drunk three times as much as they had. I just seem to be stuck on sober.

I eased off to a hallucinogenic sleep filled with crazy thoughts and encounters. I swore I never really slept completely, but then time would lapse and several hours had passed. At about 3:00 a.m., I was wide awake and ready to start my day. I got on the computer and started doing some research. I came across an article in the *LA Times* dated August 1, 2008, about how that dispensary I had visited the day before had been raided by federal agents back then. I remember thinking naively, "Oh, they must have been doing something illegal."

As the sun rose, I went for my morning run/walk and made my way back to the beach. The air was cool, and I could see my breath. After all, it was late December. Tons of homeless people walked around like zombies, asking for change. It had been a chilly night, so they were dressed in many layers. I guess they more resembled mummies than zombies.

I hung out in the room the rest of the day until 2:00 p.m., arrived then dutifully went back to the coffee shop. I had some coffee, read the paper, and waited for my meeting. This time, surprisingly, Brian showed up first.

Shortly after, Mark arrived, and Lizbeth came two minutes later. Time to sign some docs.

We sat down and Lizbeth said everything looked good as far as credit. She was ready to move forward.

Now I'm the kind of salesperson who, once they make the sale, shuts their mouth. I didn't want anything to blow this deal, but Brian decided it was his time to start asking stupid questions. I nudged him under the table. Brian could come off as rude and arrogant, and I just wanted to get the lease signed.

"When would you like the lease to begin?" Lisbeth inquired.

"How about January 15?" I stated. "That will give me time to enjoy the holidays, get packed, find a living situation, and relocate here."

"That works," she responded. With that, we filled out the lease. Mark's contribution was to add a clause that if we got shut down for any reason by a government agency, the lease became null and void. Lisbeth agreed to the amendment.

"OK, I just need a security deposit equal to one month's rent or $6,500, and we are good to go," Lizbeth announced.

I pulled out a personal checkbook and wrote out the amount. Brian asked if he could go look at the spot, so we finished up our coffees and headed across the street. Brian seemed just as excited as Mark and I were. He asked Lizbeth about the trailer, and she said she would have that moved.

I said, "You know what? Just leave it. I'm sure we could use extra storage."

"OK, that makes my life easier," Lizbeth responded.

With that, we all shook hands, and Lizbeth closed up the shop and left.

Mark was beaming with excitement, and Brian was a bit giddy as well.

"We did it!" I announced. "Let's map out what has to happen next."

We spent the next hour at the coffee shop making lists of things that needed to happen. Mark said the hardship application would be ready in about a week. I told both of them that my flight returned to Phoenix the next day at 11:00 a.m., so this would be the last time they would see me until the new year. We all shook hands and headed to our vehicles.

The night was uneventful. The next day, I returned my rental car early, and they gave me a shuttle to the airport. I arrived in Phoenix at about 1:00 p.m., losing an hour because of the time zone change. You see, Phoenix is a little unusual compared to the rest of the country, as they do not use daylight savings time. That means half the year, we are on Pacific time, and the other half, we are on Mountain time. I think they do things like that just to confuse everyone.

I got back to my house and started to make my moving plans. I had almost a month to plan the move, and we had Christmas coming up, so I didn't feel any real pressure. I had plenty of time.

Chapter 6: The Move to Los Angeles
January 2009

The holidays came and went as they always do. I spent them out in Texas with my two sisters, one of whom has Down syndrome. My stepdad also lived with them as he was now in his late seventies. My mom had passed away a few years earlier back in Michigan, and I had convinced my entire family to relocate to Texas. You see, Michigan had been declining for many years under Democrat leadership, and there were no real opportunities. My younger sister was married and had two kids, and I just thought it would be better for all involved. I had planned to move to Texas also so we could all be close, but then this California opportunity arose. I'll never forget the look on my stepdad's face when I told him what I was about to do. All he could say was, "Well, all right."

I could tell he disapproved, but again we had never been close, and I really never came to him for advice. I was already quite a bit more successful than him. In fact, I had bought the house in Texas that they were all living in, so not too much could be said. I was the gambler and risk-taker of the family. I owned a three-bedroom house in Phoenix in a downtown historic district. I had decided to rent it out for a year while I was in Texas. One set of applicants was a professional gay couple, so I decided to go with them as they were ready to move in immediately. I packed my stuff into a twenty-six-foot U-Haul, and by January 7, I was ready to hit the road. It was a five-hour drive to LA from Phoenix, so I got an early start, hoping to get there by 10:00 a.m. and miss rush hour traffic. The trip was going as planned until I got to the East LA area, and then it was gridlocked. It took me another three hours to get to my storage facility on the west side.

Once there, I had to find some helpers; fortunately, there was a Home Depot in the area. Luckily, I spoke a little Spanish as I had dated a girl from Mexico for two years while living in San Diego. As I drove into the Home Depot, I was literally swarmed by at least forty Mexicans. One even opened up the passenger door, and three jumped in. My truck was literally surrounded. I rolled down my window and told the others in broken Spanish. *"Lo siento, no mas."*

With that, we drove to the U-Haul, and, within an hour, the truck was unloaded into my unit. I dropped the workers off at the Home Depot. Come to find out none of them were actually from Mexico. They were from Guatemala. Us gringos always assume if they speak Spanish, they are from Mexico. I returned the truck to U-Haul and hailed a cab.

"The Holiday Inn, Santa Monica," I said. I had decided to stay in the same hotel just so I had my bearings.

I had booked a flight back to Arizona to pick up my truck so I had to do this all again very soon. While I was here on this trip, my goal was to find a place to live temporarily. My long-term plan was to build a three-bedroom apartment up on the loft of the dispensary. That way, I could save tons of money in rent and, at the same time, guard the product. For now, however, I needed to find a roommate situation. Again, I went to Craigslist. I could not believe the prices to rent just a single bedroom. The cheapest I found was $1,000. I wanted to stay close to the store location, so I identified two spots close by.

I called the first ad, and a man answered. We made arrangements to see it, and as I pulled up to the house, I could tell this was not the spot.

I met the guy, and he walked me around and showed me the room. The house was run down and dirty. We shook hands, and I left.

For the second location, a woman had answered with what sounded like a Hispanic accent. As I drove to her house, it was up on a hill in a much nicer neighborhood. When I pulled up, I was pleasantly surprised at the appearance of the house. It was a two-story, with what I would call a chateau look.

I knocked on the door, and an older, somewhat attractive woman answered the door.

"Hi, I'm Dalton," I announced. "Are you Anna?"

"Yes, and welcome to my house," she said enthusiastically. "Please come in."

As I entered, I noticed the house was tastefully decorated and had a pleasant aroma as incense or a candle had been burning.

"Let me show you the room," she said. We walked up the flight of stairs that were to the left of the living room. At the top of the stairs was a laundry room going forward and two bedrooms: the one on the right was Anna's room, and as I did a quick peek, I saw a bong…I mean, water pipe…on the dresser, which was a very good sign; on the left was the room Anna said was the one available. The room was small and had a single bed in it with shelves and knickknacks. I walked to the window and was surprised by the amazing view. "Is that the ocean?" I asked.

"Oh yes," she assured me. "On a clear day, you can see the ocean and at night, all the lights of the city."

I looked in the closet. It was a typical closet. There was already a dresser in the room also, so I wouldn't need to move anything from storage. "This will work," I thought.

"Can I make you a cup of coffee or perhaps some tea?" she asked.

"Yes, coffee would be nice," I replied.

"You Americans and your coffee," she said as we made our way down the steps. As we descended, I saw many photos of Anna at a much younger age. These seemed to be professional modeling pictures. She had been quite beautiful, I thought. Her age was definitely showing now, and her skin was a bit wrinkled.

We walked through the kitchen and onto a back patio with many plants. I could tell Anna was quite the gardener. She gave me a seat and offered me water while we waited for the coffee.

"Cream and sugar?" she questioned from the kitchen.

"Yes, but give me the fake sugar if you've got it," I replied. Soon, she appeared, coffee cup in hand and with a spoon and the condiments.

"So what do you think?" she asked.

"Well, I like it, especially the company," I said. "Do you live here alone?"

"Yes, just me and my cat," she said. "In my younger years, I never thought I would become the cat lady." She smiled as she contemplated her youth.

"Where are you from, if I might ask? You have a cute accent; is it Spanish?"

"No, but close. I am from Brazil, and I speak Portuguese," she responded. "But I've been here for forty years. I moved here in my twenties."

That gave me the idea that she was in her sixties, and, honestly, she looked damn good for her sixties.

"I used to be a model and a famous seamstress to the stars. I had a boutique shop on Hollywood Boulevard, and many famous people used my services," she continued.

"I saw those photos on the stairwell. You were gorgeous," I said, realizing immediately that I had just stuck my foot in my mouth.

"Yes, it's true," she said. "Many men pursued me for marriage, but I turned them all away. I was so dumb," she said, with regret in her eyes. "It's only been the last couple of years that old age has kicked in, and I lost my boutique during the financial collapse. Now I just work from home. Small orders here and there."

I could tell she had a deep sadness for days gone by. I think most women don't realize how quickly time creeps up on them. When they are young, guys trip over themselves to be with them, but, at a certain age, men's testosterone levels drop as women's looks fade. So many women end up lonely and without kids. I learned this at a dating service I had owned in Phoenix back in the late nineties before the internet took over.

"So what brought you to LA?" she asked. "You are from Phoenix, correct?"

"Yes, I am. I'm actually opening a retail store down on Venice Boulevard and Centinela, so this location is perfect. I figure it will take three months to get it open. I'm just looking for short term if that is OK."

"Yes, that is fine. What type of store?" she inquired.

"Well, I saw you have a water pipe in your bedroom, so I don't mind telling you. It's a medical marijuana collective," I said gleefully.

"Oh really?" She smiled with great interest. "I make some great brownies," she said. "Can I sell them there?"

"Ha, I'm sure we can work something out," I said as we laughed together.

"You want to smoke some?" she asked.

"No, not right now. I've got more work to do…So do I get the room?" I asked, knowing the answer already.

"I'm fine with it. Just need the first month's rent," she responded. "I've got a simple lease we can fill out."

"Great, how about I give you half now and half when I return from Phoenix in three days? I've got to drive my truck out."

She agreed. It seemed like I had just made my first friend in LA. This was going to work out well.

I now had two days to kill because I had planned on taking three days to locate housing. With that done, I figured I could start making lists of the steps needed to renovate the space. I contacted Lizbeth for the keys early and paid her the second installment of the rent lease. I spent the next couple of days measuring the space, especially the loft area, and mapping out how the apartment would look.

The days went fast, and I found myself back in Arizona. I met with my new tenants at my Arizona house, got them the keys, and was then off to California to stay. I had the same miserable drive as before, hitting gridlock at the LA border. I guess it's just something to get used to. I got into Mar Vista around 3:00 p.m. and contacted Anna. She greeted me at the door, and I made my way to my room. She had been busy sewing a dress for someone, and the living room had materials everywhere. She was definitely an industrious woman.

"It's been a long drive, and I will take you up on that smoke offer if you have any," I inquired.

"Absolutely. Come with me. All my stuff is in my bedroom," she said as she ascended the stairs. Now, she may have been a little older, but I must admit following her up the stairs in that light, little dress she had on did get my attention. She still had a model's body, I noticed.

As she entered the room, she opened a dresser and told me if I ever needed any, she kept it right there. It was nice to have that type of trust from the start.

"Oh, I would never go into your room without your permission," I promised.

"You can come into my room anytime you like," she responded confidently. "You always have my permission," she said with a little smirk. Now this made me a little uncomfortable as I really hadn't intended for any type of relationship to occur here. I wasn't quite sure what she was implying, but I was both nervous and excited at the same time. I'm sure she was an amazing lover in bed. Very sensual, I was thinking. Very erotic, I'm sure.

"OK, stop fantasizing, Dalton," I said to myself. "This is your roommate and nothing more." I decided immediately it could never be anything more than that. I needed a nice, relaxing retreat house. Not a live-in girlfriend pad, which starts out great then turns into constant bickering and expectations.

She climbed across the bed and invited me to sit down. I walked over and sat on the very edge of the bed, obviously uncomfortable. She sensed my discomfort, and things eased up a bit. We smoked a bowl, and then I went to my room to sleep. My day was done. I slept well but with a hard-on all night. I kept imagining how Anna would have been in bed. I needed to find a girlfriend and quick to avoid this temptation. Even if it was a paid girlfriend.

The next few weeks were spent getting bids on things. I had Mark and Brian walk the building with me for suggestions. Mark had suggested for security we build a man cage. I inquired what that was, and he basically told me it was a two-door cage system controlled by remote key access. It's a security door between the front lobby and the dispensary area where the drugs are sold. This would prevent would-be robbers from easy access to the drugs and cash. I liked the idea, so I got a few quotes.

I hired a general contractor to begin work on the upper balcony to build three bedrooms and a bathroom with a shower and washer/dryer hookups. No kitchen, however; this was just a crash pad. Of course, we did not even think about getting permits as that would have never been allowed in the first place. Luckily, Los Angeles is so broke they can't even police their own neighborhoods, much less send out building inspectors to every building or new business.

As I started visiting other dispensaries, I noticed a common theme. They were very sterile-looking, white offices without much decor. Their customer service was horrible, and everyone seemed stoned. It felt like you were going to the dentist's office to make a dirty drug deal. Again, from my branding expertise, I wanted to find the edge we would have over our competition.

When I picked up the local rag magazines that advertised the different dispensaries across town, they all said the same damn thing. Basically: "We have the best quality at the lowest prices."

Every ad, page after page, said the exact same thing. "Now how can this be true?" I laughed. "Only one can have the best quality, and only one can have the lowest price."

Brian was convinced that his new name "Best Bud" was a winner. He was playing off the name Best Buy, but I didn't get the connection. I could not imagine the imagery to go with that, other than a somewhat sterile store like Best Buy.

Upon doing more research, I learned that, at that time, the majority of the clients, some 85 percent, were males. So obviously having some attractive female would not hurt, right? And instead of promoting smoking pot, maybe we want to promote "natural remedies"—things that grow from the earth.

But where would they grow, I asked myself? Perhaps in a rainforest? Isn't there a big movement right now to save the rainforests? What if we created a rainforest to save the rainforests?

* * *

I asked *Brian* what he thought, and he didn't like it at all, but quite honestly I didn't care. He was just about money. I was about creating something we could be proud of.

So, there it was born. The Rainforest Collective: "Natural medicines form the earth." Now that is a theme I could have fun with. I hired a local artist to begin painting a rainforest mural on the walls. I ordered 4,000 square feet of artificial grass to put on the floor.

I met with the security company the following day. Right away, I could tell these guys were real pros.

The lead salesman's name was Aggie. I'm not sure if that was a nickname or what. I could tell he took his job very seriously and realized right away what a high-risk business this was. He identified the spot for the man cage and plotted the places for the cameras to get the most views. He recommended two cameras outside the front door and two outside in the back. He bragged that Israelis were the best in all the world at security. He mapped out everything for me and made sure we had all the features we needed on the alarms. I was getting a little worried about the price, but he said not to worry because much of this equipment could be done on a four-year lease to own. That sounded great to me. Once he had everything clear and on paper, he told me he would price things out and call me tomorrow. With that, he left.

The next few months were pretty much the same. Overseeing the build as it was occurring. I started contacting different advertising venues, including a lot of printed newspapers that you would see at the 7-Elevens.

I called the largest of the magazines, *Cannabis World*, to inquire about their rates. As I spoke to the gentleman on the phone, I came to realize that he was the owner of the magazine, so I asked if I could come down to his offices for a face-to-face meeting. I figured he would know a ton about the industry and who the major players were. He agreed, so we set up a meeting for the next day.

I arrived at the offices at 10:00 a.m. sharp as planned. His offices were located on the second floor and were easy to find. There was a reception desk in the front lobby, and I told her I was there to see Mike. She offered me water, and I had a seat.

Only a few minutes went by and Mike came bopping down the hall-way. He was a gentleman in his early forties, it appeared, and he had dark hair and a dark mustache. He came right up to me and introduced himself and told me to come with him. I followed behind, and we made our way to a corner office. It was a rather large office, with large windows and a good view. Adjoining this office was another office with a larger, heavyset man inside.

"Dalton, this is Steve," he said as Steve stood up and came to shake my hand.

"Opening a new dispensary?" he asked with some enthusiasm.

"I guess so," I smiled and shook my head. "It's a crazy new world we live in, huh?"

"Sure is, but you're getting in at the right time," he said. "Obama is set to get inaugurated next week, and once he makes his announcement, it will be the Wild West around here," he promised.

"I'll just be closing this door," Mike said to Steve.

"Nice to meet you and good luck," Steve said.

Mike motioned to the seat in front of his desk and asked me to have a seat. I did so, and he glided around his desk and sat down also. He seemed quite happy, and I guessed it was because he was in charge of sales and for once the sale was coming to him rather than him out beating the bushes visiting dispensaries.

"So what can I do for you?" he inquired.

"Well, obviously, I'm here to start an advertising campaign with you, but I also want to pick your brain about the industry in general," I proposed.

"Absolutely. We've been doing this for about six years now so we've learned a few things, I hope," he replied.

"What kind of budget do you have for advertising?" he asked directly.

Now being a salesman myself, I never answered such a question directly. It really depends on many factors. My budget should have nothing to do with his price. So I skirted the question with a question.

"Well, it really depends on what services you offer. Is it just a print magazine or do you offer an online presence and marketing? Tell me what you have," I requested.

"Well sure," he came back. "We do offer packages with online marketing, including Weed Tracker, to help people find you. What size ad were you looking for? Do you have a print-ready ad, or do you need help with graphics?" he inquired deeper.

"I definitely need help with graphics. I have the ad in my head and a few sample photos. I'm thinking a full-page ad to start, and then perhaps drop it back to a half page. I want to put some coupons at the bottom of the page, similar to some of your advertisers," I told him.

I started going into greater depth about my rainforest theme and the use of "sex appeal" in our ads. I told him about our build and hiring attractive, exotic-looking women to work at the store. He loved the idea.

"Kind of the Hooters of dispensaries," I said.

With that, we planned out our campaign, and I signed a six-month contract. I was able to purchase a front-page spot three months in advance, which I thought would give us instant notoriety. My budget with this company was $2,000 per month. I was banking heavily on its success. I left Mike's offices feeling like he had a pretty good grasp of what I wanted and that he would supply me with some sample artwork with the week he promised. With that, I headed for my newfound home at Anna's in Mar Vista.

On January 20, 2009, Barack Obama was sworn in as the forti-eth-fourth president of the US. Now, I'll be honest. I didn't vote for him. I have been a Republican my entire life. But once he was inaugurated, I supported him and I remember thinking, "Wow, racism is finally dead in the US. That's wonderful." Had I only had a crystal ball...

Barack announced shortly after his inauguration that he did not think it was a wise use of federal resources to be raiding and prosecuting medical marijuana users and growers. We all felt a great sense of relief as the raids had taken their toll on many dispensary operators. But I believed naively that if people had been getting raided, it was because they must have been going outside the law. I was soon to find out differently...Much differently.

Chapter 7: Grand Opening
February 2009

The work was progressing at an amazing rate, probably because the real estate markets were still crashing, so contractors were dying for work. The security company had given me a great lease finance plan, so for about $1,000 per month, I had the man cage, the cameras, the safe, the remote features, and the alarms. It looked like we could possibly open as early as the first week of February.

I needed to get my point-of-sale (POS) systems in place and credit card processing set up. I ordered my glass cabinets and all the packaging I needed with Mark's help and guidance. Brian was really nowhere to be seen during this whole process, other than a phone call here and there. That was OK, however. It was his job to grow the product and make sure it was ready for our opening day.

I next had to turn my attention to employees. Because I wanted to provide a different "experience" here than what I saw at other places, I decided to focus on people who were from the customer service industry (i.e., restaurants). Brian said he had a guy out in Phoenix who was a "weed expert," whatever that means, so he wanted to bring this guy out to run things. I agreed as my knowledge was limited.

I decided to run an ad on Craigslist, and I got straight to the point. I always wondered how companies like Hooters only hired the absolute hottest chicks. I mean, what did they say if an ugly chick applied, I wondered? My solution was simple. I was straight and to the point. I was looking for extremely attractive people to launch a new type of dispensary in LA. Please send a photo and resume. Bam! It paid off.

I started receiving tons of attractive applicants, both male and female.

"This interview process could be fun," I thought. "Life is good."

I began going through the emails like someone today might go through Tinder profiles. Swipe left or right. Once I had swiped all the ones I liked to the right, I dug deeper into their resume to see if they had the proper customer service experience I was looking for. Eight of the ten did, so I began to set up interviews for the upcoming Saturday. I was able to get a hold of all eight, and all of them were excited to come down on Saturday, except one. I guess she had a modeling shoot that day, so I bumped her up to Friday.

"My pleasure," I thought.

Friday came, and my first applicant came through the door. Her name was Amy, and she was twenty-five years old. I was a bit surprised at how tiny and frail she looked—somewhat anorexic. She did have a stunning face and a bubbly personality. She had also waited tables for many years at different places, so I felt she would be more than capable. I told her I would call her on Monday with my decision. I never liked to give someone a yes or no on the first meeting. I wanted to make them really want it. With that, Amy left.

Saturday, I had the seven other candidates lined up at half-hour increments starting at 10:00 a.m. The first girl to show was named Passion. She was also a very attractive young lady, about twenty-eight years old. She was also an aspiring model and had a confident attitude, great customer service experience, and management and bookkeeping experience. On a scale of one to ten, she was about a nine and a half on both looks and abilities. I figured very quickly she might become my right-hand person running the show. She demanded a little bit higher pay than the rest, but I believed she might be worth it.

The next interview was with a male named Sagi. I spoke with him on the phone, and he just had an energy about him, so I wanted to meet him. As he walked in the door, this guy beamed with energy. He was a cool, dark-skinned gentleman with quite a build and a great smile. We shook hands, and it didn't take long for us to break the ice. Definite eight on looks and experience.

Next came April, an attractive Asian lady, who was also about twenty-five. She had a great smile and tons of experience with POS systems and computers, as well as customer service. Solid seven, I thought.

Next in was Karen. She was a softer-spoken, basic white girl with purple in her hair. Six on looks and nine on abilities, I determined.

Next in was a talk, dark-haired gentleman named Eric. Great personality and tons of cash register POS experience. Solid seven.

"One more interview to go, and I'm out of here," I thought. So far, so good. I hadn't met anyone I wouldn't hire.

As I sat there reviewing the resumes, I looked up to see the most stunning girl I had seen since I had come to Los Angeles. She was about five foot five and had long dark hair. She had a tan complexion, but I could not tell if she was Hispanic or Asian or perhaps something else altogether. I thought automatically, "She's hired!" I *actually* lost the ability to speak when she approached my desk and shook my hand. It took me a second to regain my composure.

"I'm Lorraine," she said confidently as she took a seat in front of me. I was still at a loss for words, but I managed to get out my name at least.

As we talked, I saw she had very little customer service experience and was pretty much just a bookkeeper. I found out her mom was a Filipina, and her dad was from Spain, so that accounted for the unusual exotic look. All my senses as a man were still on high alert because of her sheer beauty, but after a while, I realized she just wasn't a good fit. Ten on looks but one on experience. Bummer. It would have been fun to work with her. I gave her the same feedback that I gave the others and told her I would contact her on Monday. As she walked away, my body reignited with lust for this lady. "Wow," is all I could think. It took several hours and a hot shower to get rid of that memory. "Wow."

Now, Brian had asked me if I wanted to go to Mexico with him that evening, and I thought, "What the heck."

It sounded like fun to me. Tomorrow was Sunday, so there was not much going on. Mexico was a two-and-a-half hour drive south through San Diego. Brian offered to drive, but I said no thanks to that. I didn't want the added worries of a pot-filled truck and a maniac driver. Still, I thought it was a good way for us to hang out and review our plan while blowing off some steam. Brian told me he knew of a great strip club in Tijuana that only had tens working there.

Now, I don't know about you, but the very few times I've ever peeked into a strip club in Mexico...I never saw a ten. Not even a five. But whatever, it was an interesting way to kill an evening.

We set out at about four in the afternoon. As we hit the 405 south, it was bumper to bumper but moving pretty steady. We figured we would arrive in Tijuana about 8:00 p.m. after going through security and such. We talked about the employees I was going to hire, and Brian didn't have much input. His mind was always on one subject: Money, money, money.

Once we got south of San Diego, the sun was just setting and, by the time we got close to the border, it was completely dark.

"Are you sure this is safe?" I asked. I had never gone to Mexico at night before. My mother had told me stories about street gangs looking for tourists. I mean, we lived in Michigan, for God's sake. But my mom had never been to Mexico, so how would she know anything about it?

"Oh yeah," Brian assured me. "I've been down several times at night. As long as you stay in the safe zones, you will have no issues. The police are there to protect you. You see, the clubs are owned by the cartels, and they don't want anyone messing with their customers. We are the customer, and you don't kill or rob the customer," he said.

"Makes sense," I said. I was ready for a new adventure, and it kind of reminded me of my Ukrainian romance days again. We found a paid parking space in the little border town of San Ysidro; it was in a hotel parking lot, and they charged by the hour. As we parked, a man approached our car and told us to pay $10 for four hours. We paid and began readying ourselves for our walk across the border.

Now, back in those days, nobody ever checked you as you went into Mexico, only when you were coming out. You had to walk like over a mile through a complex walkway system that crossed over the highway. There were cameras around every turn, however, presumably with American border agents monitoring in case they came across any criminals who might be trying to escape US authorities.

Brian's mood became gleeful as he explained that he always said a prayer that this not be the last time he visits Mexico. I didn't quite know how to take that, but OK then. The final step of crossing was to go through one of the barred turnstiles that only spin in one direction.

"Once you're in, there's no going back," Brian laughed as he pushed his way into Mexico. I followed dutifully. We walked down a steep sidewalk, crossed over a congested roadway, and made our way to a line of taxis.

"Taxi, taxi!" several men shouted, motioning us to their cars.

"How much to Adelita's?" Brian asked one man.

"Seven dollars," the man responded.

"No, that's too much," Brian retorted.

"OK; five dollars," the man bargained.

"Done," Brian said. With that, he told me to get in the car and we were off through traffic. The driver drove fast and didn't seem to care about pedestrians.

"I thought California drivers were bad," I thought to myself. We drove over an overpass and then down into the central part of the city. I could see the familiar clock tower located on Revolution Avenue, the typical tourist location. As we rounded a corner near a McDonalds, it was obvious we had entered into the red light district. There were literally hundreds of girls lining both sides of the streets waving at pedestrians. We turned left onto a major thoroughfare, and Adelita's neon sign dominated the street. I felt like we had just turned onto a street in Las Vegas. The driver pulled us up to the front door, and a doorman came out to greet us and open the door. Brian gave the driver his $5 and then I tipped $3 more. The driver was very happy. Brian was annoyed, but what else was new.

The doorman said, "Welcome to Adelita's," and he pushed aside the red velvet curtain that covered the doorway. As we entered, we were hit by the loud sound of American music, which made it hard to talk or hear for that matter. I turned back to see if Brian was behind me, but what I saw just shocked me. Sitting right inside the front door was a beautiful blonde sitting in a pink bikini. Our eyes met, and she gave me a big smile and a wave. I was definitely taken by surprise by her looks and, quite frankly, her white skin. I swore she was an American girl. She looked like your typical California girl but much more friendly. I saw Brian a few people back working his way through the crowd. It was standing room only. We walked toward the stage and a waiter pounced on us, asking what we would like to drink. He also asked if we would like a table and, of course, we said yes. He took us over to a table that had four young Hispanic girls sitting at it, and he motioned for them to move. They all jumped up quickly, and he began wiping down the table with a white cloth he carried on his shoulder. Once finished, he presented us with the table and we both had a seat.

"Two Pacíficos," I ordered, offering to buy the first round. Brian agreed. I looked back to the door, and the blonde was still sitting there. Our eyes met again, and she gave me a little wave.

"Oh my God, dude, that girl is hot," I exclaimed.

"Go get her," Brian said. "She seems to like you," he said with a smile.

"Nah, I need to get a couple beers in me first," I explained, still feeling shy and overwhelmed.

I surveyed the room, and there must have been at least 60 girls and an equal amount of guys walking around. The girls were either all in a row down one of the walkways or at the tables sitting with guys. Some were sitting on the guys' laps. Some were Daltoncing in front of the guys.

As far as the guys went, most were Mexican, and I only saw a couple gringos in the whole crowd. I did see a couple Asian men here and there also. That was about it. Just then, a new dancer came out on stage and our drinks arrived. We paid the waiter, and I watched as the girl walked out onto the floor with a ten-foot boa constrictor on her shoulders.

"Wow," I thought.

She began her dance very erotically with the snake as part of the whole show. It was amazing to watch her slowly "make love to the snake" while on stage. The crowd was going wild, and many guys were throwing tips on the dance stage as she proceeded to make herself known. One patron who was sitting very close to me offered her a tip, and she came right beside me as she scooped it up. The snake's head came within about a foot of my own. "What a show," I exclaimed.

Brian just sat there, very nonanimated, and stared at the girls along the walkway. Girls would come up to us and ask us if we wanted company, but we both turned them down. I ordered another beer and this time capped it with a shot of Don Julio tequila. Brian was still on his first beer, but that was fine. Once the tequila arrived, I shot it down and then chased it with salt and lime.

After two more shots of tequila, I was starting to let my guard down and began feeling the urge for company. Of all the girls in the room, I still liked the one near the front door the best, so I looked at her and waved.

Immediately, she popped up off her stool and started making her way toward my table. As she walked toward my table, her bathing suit could hardly contain her. She had on a white pair of stilettos, which accentuated every step, grinding her hips as she came. Her body was lean and athletic, and her skin was fair and smooth. She looked to be no more than twenty-five. She had an extreme confidence about her, like she knew what she had to offer.

"Do you speak English?" were the first words that came to mind.

"No, señor," she smiled as she took my hand and sat on my lap. She felt good on my lap, I must admit.

"Quieres ir?" I asked, trying to display my limited Spanish.

"Sí, amor," she said. "Let's go upstairs and drink," I was able to make out in her Spanish. She pointed upward.

"Let's go," I agreed. The waiter grabbed my drink, and she took my hand and led me toward the exit. At the door, the waiter poured my drink into a plastic cup, and he pulled out a silky red robe for the lady, which had the adult as the emblem on the back. We exited the club and entered a doorway right next door. On the way, we passed an ATM. She continued to pull me up the stairs and on the next level we reached the front desk.

"Pagar," she said, to which the man at the front desk said, "Twelve dollars." Once I had paid, he gave us a key with a room number, and she picked up a condom and some lubricant.

"My kind of service," I thought as I was still in disbelief at this whole situation. We walked toward the elevator and pushed the fourth floor button. Another couple was joining us for the ride up, a small Mexican man and an exceptionally large, young Mexican girl dressed in black lingerie. It always amazes me how other races, especially Blacks and Mexicans, like the larger heavyset girls with the big booties.

We exited at the fourth floor, and the girl walked me to the room. We passed a couple cleaning guys on the way. We opened the room, and it was like something out of a *Hustler* magazine photo shoot, with mirrored ceilings and red indirect lighting. It actually seemed very clean and upscale—not at all what I expected.

She asked me to put my donation of $80 on the table, and I complied. She dimmed the lights and turned on some music from her iPhone. We both removed our clothing, and I laid back on the bed. She started kissing my legs and made her way to my man muscle. Cleverly, she placed the condom on with her mouth and began ravaging my penis like she had not eaten in days. I was so horny I wanted to explode…and I think that's what she was going for. The one thing she didn't know is that I can never finish during oral. Once she realized this, she knew she had to mount me to complete the mission.

She moved forward and kissed my lips quickly as she plunged herself on me. Her motions were slow and grinding. This continued for a few minutes until I decided to unleash on her. I rolled her over and began thrusting her.

I actually think I had had too much tequila because I could tell I wouldn't finish any time soon. I was also a bit nervous in this situation and was having trouble maintaining my erection. Then came a knock on the door. I guess our time for the room had expired. I felt a little embarrassed that I did not finish but was ready to head back down. She dressed quickly, scooped up the money, gave me a quick peck on the cheek, and that was that. It was quite the experience for my first time in Mexico and still worth the $80 bucks, I thought.

When I got back downstairs, Brian had already been up and back. He was standing by the front door and appeared ready to go.

"How was it?" he asked.

"Not what I expected," I replied, still feeling embarrassed I could not complete the mission.

"You ready?" he asked.

"Ready for what? We just got here," I replied.

"Yeah, well, I've got a busy day tomorrow. We've completed our mission here," he stated.

"We drove four hours to spend an hour in a bar, then drive four hours back?"

"Yup, let's go," he said. I couldn't argue; he was determined. I had just found the happiest place on Earth, and I was there with a stick in the mud.

"I'll be back, I promise," I thought, now that I knew how it worked. "And without Brian," I noted.

With that, we made our way back to LA. On the way, I had a lot of time to think about the experience I had just had. I'm sure there a lot of people thinking, "Oh my God, you are taking advantage of these young girls," but I really have to explain something. In that situation, they are the predator, and we are the prey. The average police officer makes $300 per month in Mexico, I found out. One of these girls brings in that amount each night. This enables them to send money to their families and live a "movie star" lifestyle. As far as the sex is concerned, I've found that 80 percent of them are enjoying it more than I am.

"But what about sex trafficking?" many do-gooders ask. Yes, I'm sure it happens, but most of the girls I have met seem very independent and in control of their own decisions. Their body, their choice, right? Our society has much more important issues to worry about than the oldest profession. It's never going away as long as there are men with money and women that want that money. I feel absolutely no guilt in helping a lady pay her bills while enjoying her company. It is a win/win…so get over it.

Brian dropped me off at Anna's and went off to do whatever Brian does. He said he need to go to the grow.

"Now that's commitment," I thought, as I hit the bed.

Sunday turned to Monday, and that was the day I had planned to hire my crew. I got a hold of each person, and they were extremely excited. I tried to call Lorraine to give her the bad news, but she did not pick up. I just told her to call me when she could and left it at that.

I invited all the new hires to a training meeting that coming Friday, and they were all able to make it. The construction was pretty much finished, and the wall mural guy was completing his masterpiece—a rainforest complete with animals, a waterfall, and even an Incan tomb where the medicine man lived. Everything was taking shape. Mark started inviting growers down to the store so they could display their goods to me. I planned on not buying a lot of outside weed as Brian had what he claimed to be the best OG in LA, which was a pretty big statement. Our grand opening was planned for the first Monday in February. I figured a Monday was best so we could work the kinks out first.

By Friday we were completely ready to go, and the trainees all showed up at 10:00 a.m. completely excited. Now, I always like to play a few ice-breaker games so people can get to know each other, and everyone seemed to enjoy them. Then we looked at scheduling and positioning. There were front of the house and back of the house positions, or admin and "bud tenders" as we called them, as a play on the word "bartender."

The front of the house worked on building client files and verifying IDs and the back of the house worked on the POS system and weighing our product. They were also in charge of rolling joints in their free time as we gave those to new patients.

Passion positioned herself in the front of the house. She was a natural with the database and figured it out quickly. April, the Asian girl, joined her, as well as Karen, the blonde with the purple streak. Eric would be our daytime bud tender, and Sage and Amy both were scheduled for nights. I figured Brian and I could jump back and forth to help where need.

"Hey, where is Brian, anyway? Shouldn't he be here?" He had been invited. Probably another edible got him. We spent the good part of six hours getting everything ready.

It was here! We were now ready to open.

Afterward, I invited everyone over to the neighborhood bar called the Good Hurt to have a couple drinks and get to know each other better. I could feel we were all gelling into one big family.

At the Good Hurt, when we arrived, the place was relatively empty. So, we all bellied up to the bar, and I ordered a round of drinks for everyone. The bartender was a young female dressed in what appeared to be a maid outfit. Her hair was platinum blond, and she had bright red lipstick. She also had a mole on her right cheek, which looked like it had been highlighted. Honestly, she looked like a Marilyn Monroe imitator. The bar was designed to kind of have the look and feel of the 1950s, so she seemed to fit right in. We grabbed a couple tables and pushed them together to fit all of our eight guests. The waitress showed up and asked if we wanted to order any appetizers, so I ordered a variety of foods, including some nachos, quesadillas, and mozzarella sticks. There was a great energy in the group, and it seemed like Eric and April were hitting it off exceptionally well. Sagi was entertaining everyone on the other end of the table with his bigger-than-life personality, and I was sitting next to Passion, who really seemed to be a take-charge type of person.

The waitress returned with the plates and napkins and asked where we were all visiting from. I announced proudly that I was opening a dispensary a few doors down.

"Oh really? That's awesome," she exclaimed.

"I'll be your best customer," she promised. "If you ever give out free apples, keep me in mind…Hey, I want you to meet the owner here; he's back in the kitchen."

A few minutes later, she emerged with a tall, good-looking guy with dark hair and blue eyes. I stood up to shake his hand and introduce myself.

"Hi, I'm Jason," he announced.

"So you're opening up a dispensary?" he inquired.

"Yes, just a few doors down, next to the Chinese restaurant," I replied.

"Nice! Did you know that Chinese restaurant was in the movie *Rush Hour* with Jackie Chan?" he asked me.

"No, I did not," I replied, barely remembering the movie. Since that time, I looked it up and sure enough. It was labeled Chinese and Soul food just for the movie, however.

"Yeah, it was a pretty big deal a few years ago," he said. "Well, I might be down to visit you also," he promised.

"That would be great! Anytime," I said. We exchanged phone numbers and that was that for our first meeting. After about 5:00 p.m., happy hour ended, and we all made our way toward the door.

"Well, you all have your schedules for next week, so we will see you then," I announced. With that, we all parted ways. I did notice Eric and April walking together deep in conversation. A new "office" romance, I suspected? Oh well, we're all adults, I thought.

I made my way back to Anna's house for the last night. You see, tomorrow was moving day, and Brian and I were moving into the three-bedroom apartment we had constructed. Anna seemed sad to see me leaving, but she did understand. She offered to provide living plants and a cleaning service for the shop, and I took her up on the offer. I thought that was a great way for us to stay in contact.

Once I got to my room, I received a text from Lorraine, the girl I had decided not to hire. She had never called me back so I assumed she wasn't interested. Her text was a little confusing at first. She basically said, "Hey, what's up," and I informed her that all the hiring had been done.

"That's cool," she said. "I'm really busy at work right now anyway, but I was excited about working with those pretty blue eyes of yours," she stated.

This comment took me by surprise. I remembered how attractive she was and how I had lost the ability to talk at our first meeting. I never in a million years thought this beautiful young lady would be interested in a guy fifteen years her senior, but the words were pretty leading. Now it's much easier to be brave via text, so I decided to pursue. My heart was thumping as I typed the next words.

"Well, that doesn't mean we can't hang out sometime," I suggested with a lump forming in my throat.

"Yeah, we could do that," she replied. "Hit me up next weekend, and we will see if you have any game," she said.

I tried to play it cool with her and not seem too anxious, so I said, "Yeah, we will see what happens."

Then I said, "We have our grand opening next week, so I'm not sure how busy I'll be." I put it out there, hoping beyond hope this was not the case.

"Well, just hit me up if you want to hang," she said.

"Sounds good," I replied, and that was that. My heart was racing.

"Wow, I'm loving LA," I thought.

The next day, I had two guys move my things. I again rented a U-Haul, and we set up beds and furniture in the upper bedrooms. Brian was supposed to bring his product down so we could have some more product than just the original stock I had purchased from Mark's vendors. I had purchased a variety of strains, and Brian said he had three additional strains. As I was finishing up the move, Brian showed up with his dog and walked up to his room, where he locked the dog in the room. I asked him where the strains were and told him we needed to get those weighed out. Then he shocked me with his reply.

"Yeah, I've been meaning to bring that up. I had to sell my flower to The Farmacy. They paid me $4,000 per pound. I really need the money to pay some bills. I'm getting ready to lose my house in Arizona," he stated.

"Really, Brian? Really? I have put tens of thousands of dollars out, and the only thing you were bringing to the table was your flower. Now you don't even have that?" I was thoroughly pissed off.

"I can have another crop ready in three months," he offered.

"And how about my money you owe me? Remember the $10,000?" I asked.

"Well, now that we are partners, can we just leave that invested in the business?" he suggested.

"Oh, you are going to invest more of *my* money in the business, are you? This is total bullshit, Brian, and you know it."

"Well, tomorrow we are opening, so you can take the money out of our sales," he proposed.

"So I'm going to pay back my money to myself with the work and investment I have made? Nice, Brian. Nice. Not a good way to start a partnership, Brian."

With that, I walked down the stairs and out of the building. I decided to go back to the Good Hurt and calm down. I was very upset with Brian. I felt like I had been lied to the entire time. When I arrived, I was greeted by the same waitress who, come to find out, was the owner's girlfriend. I sat up at the bar and the same Marilyn Monroe bartender was there with another bartender. Both were dressed in the "French maid" outfit.

"You again," she said with a smile. "I heard you were opening a dispensary soon."

"Yup, we are opening tomorrow," I informed her.

"Well, your first drink is on me," she offered, "and just let me know if you ever want to hang out down there; I'll give you my number."

What I started to realize very quickly was that owning a pot shop in LA was almost like being a rock star. Everyone wanted to "hang out."

"How late are you working tonight?" I inquired, wondering if tonight could become very interesting.

"Oh, I don't get done until 2:00 a.m." She frowned.

"Ah yeah, I'm heading to bed early tonight. Big day tomorrow."

"Any time, just let me know," she promised. With that, I finished my second drink and walked back to the store. When I got there, Brian had already left. I could hear his dog in his bedroom scratching and clawing at the door.

"That's great for the new construction," I thought.

With that, I hit the sack. It felt like Christmas Eve. I was so excited I could barely sleep. After an hour of not sleeping, I walked down to the dispensary and popped often some Grape Ape, a purple strain that helps you sleep. One of the few things I had learned so far about the product was indicas are for the nighttime, and sativas are for daytime use. The indica kicked in quickly, and I drifted into another hallucinogenic dream world filled with beautiful blondes and boa constrictors. Most dreams are just reliving what you experienced that day or days prior. This was turning into quite an adventure, and we had not even opened gifts yet.

* * *

The next day, Passion and Eric showed up at about the same time, and April showed up shortly after. Eric was going to be my full-time daytime bud keeper, and Passion was in charge of the girls out front. The girls wore flower ring dresses, and Eric sported a Hawaiian shirt as instructed.

At 10:00 a.m., we opened the doors…and crickets. Nobody showed. Eleven o'clock, nobody. Twelve o'clock, nobody. At about noon, someone popped their head in and asked if we were a smoke shop, which we were not. He didn't have a doctor's recommendation so he couldn't buy anything. The whole day was the same. Not one customer. The phone rang several times, with people inquiring about us. Also there were a lot of sales people. About 5:00 p.m., our night crew showed up. Sagi came in as well as Amy; I reported the dismal results and promised things would pick up. Karen showed up a few minutes later, and Passion instructed her further on the front-end operations.

At about 5:15 p.m., a young man poked his head in the door and asked if he could see the owner. He had a backpack on his back, so we went to our "smoke room," which was an area dedicated to clients who wanted to partake on site. You see, the rules and laws were so undefined at this time, we felt we could get away with a lot. Once we entered the room, the young man proceeded to open up his pack and display his product. It turned out he was a grower from the "Emerald triangle," which was a region in Northern California that claimed to have the best marijuana growers in the world. You see, they had been perfecting their strains for many decades and had turned it into both an art and a science.

The strain he presented was called "headband," and he also had some "chem dog." He was most proud of his third strain, however, which he called LA Confidential. Under examination, all the stains looked amazing, but I explained to him that our first day was slow, so I was hesitant to buy any more until things picked up.

"No worries," he said. I can leave them on consignment and check back in a week.

"That works," I said. With that, we drew up a consignment form and he left a quarter pound of each. I was glad to replace the strains Brian had promised then reneged on. I still was so mad about that whole situation.

About 5:30 p.m., we got our first true customer, who said she lived right down the block. A couple of young guys stopped in to register and get the free joints that we offered but didn't buy anything. Three or four more customers stopped in throughout the rest of the night and when we closed the drawer, we had done a whopping $250 in sales. I'm not gonna lie. I was more than worried, but I had to put on a positive front for my new employees.

"Well, that's to be expected," I promised. As they left, I went up to my apartment to lick my wounds. Brian called, and I reported the sad news. He didn't say much, and I barely wanted to talk to him.

"Did you take your dog out today?" I inquired. "I don't want that new carpet getting ruined by a fucking dog."

"No, I'll be by later," he promised. "He's got doggy pads to go to the bathroom on."

"OK," I said, still so disappointed in our first day.

The week got progressively busier but still nothing to get excited about. I was banking on the weekend to turn things around, but each day we only did about $500 a day. We did about $2,500 total for the entire week, which was barely enough to cover rent and utilities, much less employee wages and product. The next week was similar without much growth. I contacted my advertiser Mike to find out if there was anything else I could be doing.

Mike suggested I do a giveaway. It seems another dispensary had given away a hundred free eighths of different strains of flower, and they had lines forming around the block.

"I'm willing to try anything," I agreed.

We began to make our plans for this big promotion. We planned it for a Saturday to get maximum affect. I planned to give away one hundred free eighths, followed by one hundred free grams, then one hundred free joints. You just had to register into our database. All other product was half off, including our edibles.

Chapter 8: The Big Bang
March 2009

The weeks went by, and we promoted the hell out of the giveaway, online and on the front page of the magazine.

When the Saturday arrived, about an hour before the store opened, I saw a line forming outside. My employees snuck in the back door because the long line that had now formed was actually bending around the block. I called some other employees to come in and called Brian for help. The employees agreed, so we had everyone working by the time we opened the doors. It felt like the Black Friday right after Thanksgiving. The rush was on. It was amazing what free weed could generate. For the next hour upon hour, we were overrun by new patients, filling out paperwork and ushering them into the back room. Even Brian showed up and was able to help facilitate somewhat. Most people were just here for the free weed, but many also purchased additional items. By the end of the day, we were out of half of our product and had generated about $2,500 in additional sales. More importantly, we now had over three hundred people in our database, who we could now market specials to. Our store closed at 10:00 p.m., and everyone was completely exhausted. Sagi suggested we all head to the Good Hurt and a few agreed, but I told him I was hitting the sack early. It had been a long day. I asked my Sunday employees to come in early for restocking and cleaning. We had gotten our ass kicked today, but honestly, I thought we handled it quite well.

I hit my bowl and went up the bedroom. Brian was planning to stay for the first night, and I told him to take his damn dog out. I offered to help with the dog, but he said again that his dog bites and doesn't like people. I thought that was odd. Most dogs liked me.

"Maybe another day," I thought.

With that, I hit the bed and was out like a light.

Morning came quickly and my employees, specifically Eric and Karen, showed up early. I had asked April and Sage to be on call just in case. We began vacuuming and cleaning. The place was a mess. I even called Anna to come help and bribed her with free weed. She showed up ten minutes earlier to help.

At ten, we opened the door and there were already a few people waiting. Many expressed regret at not making it yesterday, and I made sure everyone got a free gift. Sundays, we closed early at 8:00 p.m., but we had done over $1,000 in sales. Things were definitely looking up. I began to relax.

As I went upstairs, I got a text from Lorraine, telling me she was off tomorrow if I wanted to hang out. I tried to call her, but it went straight to voicemail. I'm still a little old school and would rather talk than text, but the younger people prefer just the opposite, so I obliged.

"Yeah, we can hang out tomorrow. Why don't you stop by the shop about five?" I suggested.

"I'll take you out for dinner and drinks," I offered.

"Sounds good," she said, "I still need to see if you got game."

"Interesting girl," I thought.

Monday was quite a bit busier than the previous week, and everyone was still buzzing about our free giveaways. I had installed a "Wheel of Fortune" in the dispensary; every person who spent over $25 got a free spin of the wheel. They could win papers, joints, or the luckiest person could win an eighth of their choice. People really enjoyed a game of chance. Again, my goal was to engage as many senses as possible. My night crew had just begun showing up at 5:00 p.m. when I received a text from Lorraine.

"I'm outside," she texted.

"Well, come in," I suggested, wanting to show off my hot date to my employees.

"No, I'm good," she said. "If you want to cancel, we can cancel."

"No, I don't want to cancel," I responded, a little thrown off guard by her abrupt response.

I informed my employees I was leaving and that Brian would be here for closing. With that, I walked out the front door and began searching for Lorraine. She popped out of a car, parked at one of the meters. She was on the phone with someone but waved me over. She was just as hot as I remembered. She remained on the phone while I took her by the hand and led her to my truck. I opened her door for her and couldn't help but notice her perfect ass as she hoisted herself into my passenger seat. She was wearing a white blouse tied in the middle and a short skirt. Her legs were firm and sexy.

I walked to the driver's side and jumped in the driver's seat. She had gotten off the phone and gave me a look of inquiry.

"So, do you like any sports?" she asked as if this were a deal-breaker question.

"Just one," I replied, not being an addict of all sports.

"Which one?" she inquired.

"Well, I like the NFL," I replied.

"Who is your team?" she asked, even more interested.

"The Denver Broncos," I replied. You see, I had lived in Denver when Elway won his first Super Bowl. Before that, I was more of a college football fan as I grew up in Notre Dame territory.

"YOU LIKE THE DONKEYS?!" she exclaimed in fake disgust.

"Oh no," I said. "Uh oh. You're not a fucking Raiders fan, are you?" I retorted. Only one type of fan would call the Broncos, the donkeys.

"Damn straight until I die," she said. "Look at my car." A huge Raider emblem was on the back window.

"Well, I guess we can cancel this date right now," I said jokingly. "I'm a Raider hater from way back."

"Is that what you want to do?" she asked as she reached for the door handle.

Now, I was looking at one of the most erotic, sexy young women I had ever seen and the very last thing I wanted her to do was get out of my car, but I had to play it cool. Because I really just thought she was "testing my game," as she had put it several times.

"Nah, you drove all the way here," I said. "I think we should give this a shot."

"Whatever, then let's go already," she retorted. I think we were both glad it was continuing, and I also think I had passed her first test. I wasn't an ass kisser or beta boy just trying to get some. I was a player, and she was my game. Or was it the other way around? I was not sure yet but was excited to find out.

I drove her to the Santa Monica Pier and told her we were eating at Bubba Gump. A girl like this likes a guy who makes decisions. We got to the restaurant and there were three very attractive hostesses at the front desk. They took us to our table and we took our seats.

"Can I put your first drink order in?" the hostess asked.

"Ah sure, what would you like?" I asked Lorraine.

" A beer is fine," she said. "What are you having?"

Now normally I would get a shot of Jack with a beer chaser, but I was feeling like I was on vacation, so I was thinking about a Long Island iced tea.

"Oh, is that your girly little frou-frou drink?" she asked with a sarcastic grin.

"Did you want a pineapple and a little umbrella too, sissy boy?" she asked with a blistering attack. I burst out laughing.

"Fuck you, Raider bitch" is all I could come up with. "You're just mad 'cause the Broncos have beat you like eight times out of ten in our last meetings," I came back swinging.

We both held our fake poses and when the waitress came back, I ordered her beer and my frou-frou drink. I made sure to ask if they could put a little umbrella in it, and the waitress agreed. I smirked at Lorraine, letting her know I would not be intimidated and would drink whatever the fuck I wanted.

"Are you hungry?" I asked with a slight smartass tone.

"Well, that is why we came to a restaurant, isn't it?" she said, giving me the same smartass tone back.

"Do you like shrimp?" I asked.

"Love it," she replied, so I ordered a big bucket along with some crab cakes. When our drinks arrived, Lorraine started in again with the girly drink stuff and told me next time I should just wear a dress.

I told her, "Anyone can drink a beer, but how about a shot?"

"Bring it," she said, "I'm not a lightweight."

"Can you handle whiskey?" I asked, "Or are you Raider fans too wimpy?"

"Whatever you've got, I can handle," she stated.

Our food arrived quickly and our shots shortly after. We continued to ride each other about football and drinks. We both had a good appetite for both food and more shots. Two more shots later, Lorraine started giving me more shit about the Broncos, so I decided to shut her up by grabbing the back of her head and burying my tongue in her mouth. She didn't resist, and we made out for several minutes, oblivious to the people around us. The whole mood had changed, and I held one of her hands as my other hand started exploring her thigh underneath the table.

The waitress came with the check, and we both stood up and walked toward the door hand in hand.

The hostess looked at me and said, "Now you take care of her."

"Oh, I will," I said as we walked out into the night.

"I have a blanket and some weed in the car," I said. "Let's go down below the pier and smoke out," I suggested.

She agreed and I gave her another deep kiss, pulling her sexy body closer to mine. We grabbed the blanket and the weed and walked down a sandy pathway that led below the pier. The sun had just set and the Ferris wheel lights had just started flashing red, blue, and yellow.

We found a spot under the pier, and I laid out the blanket. We both sat down and began making out again. I just couldn't believe how beautiful this girl was and how this was all coming together so quick. After a few minutes, I pulled away and started packing the pipe. We kissed a few times, and then I lit it up. We both took long, hard drags. I decided to push ahead and laid her back on her back as we kissed. I positioned a leg on top of her legs then slid my body into a missionary position, yet fully clothed. I grinded her into the sand, and she returned the motion.

Then she said, "Hold on," and she pushed me to get off. I figured that I had maybe gone a little too far, and I was fine with that. I just felt lucky to be here, making out with a beautiful young lady by the ocean. The carnival lights flashed all around us.

To my surprise, Lorraine unzipped my pants and pulled me out. "I'm gonna make you really hard," she promised. With that, she began an amazing oral demonstration.

I must say I was very surprised and a little nervous as people were walking up and down the beach. I saw four teenagers approaching, but it was dark enough that I didn't think they could see exactly what was happening.

Once I was good and hard, she asked if I was ready for it, and all I could do was say, "Yes."

She pushed me backward so I was in a sitting position and climbed on top, pushing her panties to the side. I entered her warm tight pussy that was extremely wet. Now, from any observer's standpoint, she was just sitting on my lap with a skirt on, but I was deep inside of her, and it felt amazing.

She whispered, "Let me get mine first," which I took to mean she wanted to come first, so I let her do her thing. She knew how she wanted it. After several minutes, I could tell she was ready to orgasm and she did, all over me. I was still hard as fuck and ready to take my turn when a beach security vehicle started to approach us at a rapid pace. I remained inside her because there just wasn't time to move. I took the pipe and buried it in the sand with my right hand. The vehicle turned on a spotlight and shone it directly at us. Now, I was a forty-year-old adult and, to be honest, I had never been arrested for anything in my life. I wasn't sure if what we were doing was a crime but if it was take me away, officer. Guilty as charged. I don't know too many single men that could have turned this down, and I sure as hell wasn't going to. I could imagine trying to explain it to a judge.

"Just *look* at her. What's a man supposed to do, your honor?" That would be my total defense.

I leaned over and looked right at the security officer and said, "Is there a problem, sir? Can you turn off the damn light?"

He said, "Are you OK, ma'am?" to Lorraine, to which she replied, "Yes, now turn off the light, please."

He did and then drove away, but I could see he was circling around so I figured it was time to get mine now before he returned. I laid Lorraine back on the blanket and began to pummel her without mercy. I was just able to finish before the truck returned. As we straightened out our clothing, I noticed that the four teenagers had been watching us the whole time from behind.

"Hope we gave them a show," I thought.

We packed up our things and went back to the truck. It was the best first date I had ever had in my life.

"Damn, I love LA," I thought.

She dropped me off at my dispensary and said she had to go. I asked if I would see her again, and she said maybe.

"Don't get all girly and want to hang out all the time," she said. "I'm not ready for that."

"I can't believe I like a donkey's fan," she said as she drove away.

"Well, I think that went well," I surmised.

"My God, I love LA," I thought as I walked to my room. I felt so used…

Chapter 9: Trouble on Two Fronts
April 2009

February turned to March, and March turned to April. Business was steadily increasing so I added a few staff members. Passion brought one of her friends in, Cindy, a very attractive and smart girl who was very flirtatious. Another young lady named Brittany came in, who was twenty-two years old and loved to show off her body. She wore a low cut pair of shorts with the top of the G-string protruding out. I also hired another guy as I didn't like the girls to be left alone, especially at nights. Marco was a nice Hispanic gentleman who had lost half a hand in an accident. He always wore a glove on that hand so people didn't stare. I was really never sure how much of his hand was missing. I also hired another young man named Joshua. He told me he was a very experienced grower, which was great because I was thinking we needed to start growing our own stuff at some point. The upstairs apartment had two spare bedrooms, so that might be the perfect start for a grow. But then again, if we ever got raided, we would lose everything, so I realized I might have to put some more thought into that.

I worked Friday nights and Brian worked Saturdays, but he really wasn't that proficient at anything. He sure did love counting the money at the end of the night, however. I was still very pissed that he hadn't contributed anything to the deal and was benefiting from all my work and investment. I told him he wouldn't get any pay until I was fully reimbursed.

I was sitting in the front lounge one Saturday night when a couple of Black thugs walked in the door. These guys definitely looked out of place as far as Mar Vista was concerned. They walked to the front desk and asked for Brian. Brian came out from the back and saw the two guys and invited them to go upstairs with him to our apartment. About a half hour later, the two came walking down with a duffle bag full of stuff and walked right out the door.

I walked directly upstairs and confronted Brian.

"Who the hell was that?" I asked.

"Are you selling drugs out the back door illegally?" I asked him directly.

"I owed these guys some money," he said, "so I paid them with weed."

I went ape shit. "Brian, those were gang bangers and you invited them to our store? What the hell were you thinking? Don't you ever do any type of drug deal here, or I will call the cops on you myself. Do you got me? You fucking asshole."

"Got it," he said.

"And you paid them with the weed you are supposed to be supplying to the shop?" I asked.

"Only part of it; I still have some."

"Damn it, Brian, you never keep your deals!"

I left the store and walked down to the Good Hurt before I put some hurt on Brian.

May 2009

The next day was Sunday, and I decided to reconcile the books with the inventory. When I compared the inventory to what the actual inventory was, there was quite a discrepancy. I spent the rest of the day going through the numbers and, as best I could tell, there was about $10,000 missing. That was a lot since we were barely starting our third month.

I was pissed. There was only one person who had that kind of access beside me. Brian came home about 5:00 p.m. that day, and I just unleashed on him. I accused him of stealing the money and demanded he move out of the building immediately. I told him this was not a request, and he had better start packing his shit and his dog and go. As I walked toward the door, Brian grabbed me and stepped in the way. I exploded. My immediate reaction sent Brian flying across the room. He was smaller than me and much weaker. He jumped back up and came toward me again, but my look made him think twice.

"You get the hell out of here now, or I'm calling the cops and reporting your grow," I said.

"I didn't steal the money," he promised.

"I don't care, Brian. It's missing. Whether you stole it or just lost it, I don't care. You need to go."

"I shouldn't have to leave," he said. "This is my business also."

"Oh, really? What have you contributed?" I asked in disgust.

"Well, it was my idea," Brian came back.

"Yes, it was your idea," I agreed. "Big fucking deal. Get out now, or I'm calling the cops." I started to dial the phone.

"OK, I'm going," he said.

"Can I come back for the dog?" he requested.

"Yes, but you have to leave your key."

Brian grabbed his stuff and went to the door. "This is bullshit; I didn't steal anything," he repeated.

"Just go!" I said. So he left. I immediately changed the passcodes on the bank accounts and the security systems. I was glad to be done with Brian. He added no value here. His illegal activity could end me in jail.

"Good riddance," I thought.

Brian called a few days later to plead his case. He offered to take a lie detector test to prove his innocence. I reluctantly agreed.

A few days later, we were sitting in front of the lie detector and Brian was answering a series of questions. The test was being administered by a young lady. I got to sit next to her and watch the needle's reaction as Brian was asked the questions.

"Have you stolen any money from the company?" was the first question. He said, "No." The needle went crazy.

"Have you stolen any marijuana from the company?" Brian said no and the needle went crazy.

"Are you currently lying about your theft?" Brian said no, and the needle went crazy.

Once the test was complete, Brian jumped up, very confident he had passed. The tech informed him that he had failed miserably. His face deflated.

"It's not true," he said.

"I didn't steal anything," he repeated.

"Well, the test says you did, Brian, so that's good enough for me." I walked toward the door.

"I need to take another test," he begged. This one had cost $300, but something in his body language made me think something wasn't right. He seemed sincere, and I considered myself an excellent read on people.

"Well, set it up Brian, but you're paying for the next one," I promised.

Brian did set up another one. This time, it was $600. We got the same results. Fail, fail, fail.

"We're done, Brian," I said as I left the building.

"I don't understand," Brian said. "I know I didn't take anything."

A few days later, Brian called me again, wanting to set up another test.

"Brian, man, come on. How many times are we gonna go through this?"

"Well, I was talking to a lie detector expert and he said the previous ones were flawed," he said. They had been done all wrong. I should not have been in the room during the test.

I listened and again told him to set it up.

This time, Brian set up a very serious testing. He chose a company that had done the lie detector case of Larry Flynt from *Hustler* magazine. This test cost $1,500, and I was not allowed in the room or even to witness it from a window. They said that it would cause "undue anxiety." The woman was very confrontational with me and told me the other lie detectors were bogus. I sat in the waiting room for about forty-five minutes and then Brian returned with a report and a smile. The report showed he had passed. I asked the test administrator how this could be, and she said that he was innocent, period. I really didn't like her attitude with me. I was the one who had taken the losses.

At this point, I really didn't know what to believe, but the bottom line, the one thing for sure, was that the money was missing. Whether it be from gross incompetence or theft really didn't matter. I told Brian we were finished. I was generous enough to give him a five-year promissory note that stated that if the store became successful, I would pay him $50,000 to buy him out. I didn't want to work with him anymore anyhow. Too much bad blood.

April 2009

It was toward the end of April, and I was sitting in the front lounge of the store when a mail person walked through the doors asking for me. When I walked over to the person, he gave me a certified letter from the city of Los Angeles. When I opened it, I was given a cease and desist letter from the district attorney's office. Stephen Cooley was the district attorney at the time. I was ordered to close my doors immediately or risk fines and/or jail time. I was in shock. Just when things seemed to be going well, this happened. I was given until June 7 to close my doors or risk being fined and/or arrested.

I immediately contacted Mark, my consultant, and he told me that the letters had been going out to all the hardship exemptions. The district attorney was trying to bully people into closing. The city attorney had again resumed their raids, despite the promise of Obama not to use their resources to go after dispensaries. It seemed the LA police department (LAPD) were working in conjunction with federal agents to shut down the "scourge" of renegade dispensaries that had opened under the hardship clause. The reality is the Drug Enforcement Agency (DEA) didn't like us cutting into their profits, I surmised.

Regardless, this threw my whole mindset into a spiral. I had over $300,000 invested in this store, and I wasn't going to go down without a fight. Mark's advice was to get an attorney involved and pull as many dispensaries together to fight the city's actions. He recommended I start going to the LA City Council meetings to voice my opinion and meet other people involved in the fight. I thought these were both great ideas.

I began searching the internet for attorneys who could possibly defend me. Mark had recommended a few, and I had went to their offices, but nobody really impressed me. I called one on the phone, and he agreed to actually come to my dispensary and talk about the issues. We set up an appointment for the next day, and he showed up at the scheduled time.

Very quickly, I determined this person was an arrogant money chaser and really had no idea what to do in the situation. He sat on my couch, with a leg draped over the arm, trying to impress me with his knowledge and physique. As the conversation went on, he listed off all the reasons I could never beat City Hall, but then told me I would need come up with $250,000 to even try.

Now I don't know how much you know about hiring attorneys, but I've often found that most of them are very book smart but not very street smart. Most have lots of facts and information in their heads, but actually getting things done is a different story. Usually, what they do best is send you invoices for their time…what a racket. It's one of the few professions you can charge an arm and a leg for and not guarantee results. I had learned at a much earlier time, in a legal situation, that you do not hire an attorney to advise you what to do. You hire an attorney to do what you want them to do in in the most legal way possible. I could tell this big swingin' dick wasn't going to accomplish much.

The following week, I decided to go to my first LA City Council meeting. Their main agenda that week was to hear from the citizens about their concerns with medical marijuana. So I put it on my calendar. I also decided to go talk to some nearby dispensary owners to see what they were planning to do.

As I entered the neighboring dispensary, I saw a young African American gentleman talking to the two store owners, who were some young guys with a very friendly attitude. As I approached them, I introduced myself and soon found out that the gentleman's name was David

Welch, and he was an attorney in Los Angeles who had just started his practice a couple years prior. It seemed he had had the same idea to go talk to dispensary owners and see what they were planning on doing, as well as to offer his assistance. I liked that an attorney was out beating the streets looking for business. That told me he did not mind working for a living.

We all had a talk about how outraged we were to receive those closure letters and what we planned to do about it. Mr. Welch told me in legal terms why the city was way out of line with these letters and had no legal cause to enforce them, which was music to my ears.

He said he had to leave shortly so we exchanged business cards for more discussion later. I went to visit a few more dispensaries that afternoon to start building up a little support group. I'm not gonna lie, I was scared. My lifetime savings was tied up in this project, and I had just been ordered to shut down by the district attorney of Los Angeles. That night, I did not sleep well. I had continuous nightmares about being shut down or, worse, raided. I decided to eat a brownie to help me sleep.

Chapter 10: The LA City Council

June 2009

It was Tuesday morning, and the council was going to begin its meeting about the medical marijuana issue and had invited public comment. I was both excited and nervous to go to my first meeting. I had never been to the downtown area before and I decided to take my motorcycle. You see, in California, it was legal to split lanes while driving a bike, so that meant you could bypass the heavy traffic and cruise right down the middle. Now, at first, when I saw riders doing this, I thought it was absolutely fucking crazy. Motorcycles were coming within inches of the side mirrors of cars and trucks. Sometimes those big ass mirrors of pickup trucks would come within an inch. I thought there was no way in hell you would ever catch me doing that. But after driving for several months in the gridlocked traffic, my whole attitude had changed, and I was zipping along between cars like the best of them. People often asked me if I was scared to drive a motorcycle and my answer was this: "If you think about it, it is the only time I really feel alive. Every decision could possibly be life and death." With the wind flying past me and the sights and the sounds, I absolutely loved it.

Still, traffic was thick, and it took me about an hour to get to the city building. Now I noticed what I assumed was the city building. A tall, magnificent building with a marble-looking exterior. I could tell this building had some history to it. I drove around for another half hour hoping to score a parking meter, but most limited you to an hour. Finally, I had no choice and settled for the hour. I walked around the building looking for the entrance and soon discovered it was on the exact opposite side of the building. I scurried along quickly, trying to get to the chambers on time.

Once I found the main door, I realized I wasn't the only one showing up for the meeting. There were a good thirty people in front of me going through the metal detectors. In the line were businessmen with briefcases, probably attorneys, and a lot of hippie-looking people and just normal folks like myself.

When I got to the metal detector, I emptied my pockets and walked through the arched detector. Of course a buzzer went off. The officer pointed at my belt buckle and had me remove it. My second attempt to enter was successful. Once through, everyone made their way to the elevators like cattle being led to a slaughter. I managed to barely squeeze into one of the elevators, which took us to the third floor. Inside, the room was quite full. People were rushing around trying to find seats. I decided to sit in the back and observe. I notice in the very back row was an extremely attractive blond lady who seemed to be sitting alone, so I decided to work my way in that direction. Luckily, there was a seat right next to her so I asked if it was taken and she said, "No, go right ahead."

I sat down just as the proceedings began. In the front of the room, all the council members were taking their seat and one man stood up and said, "Let this meeting come to order." As the meeting was coming to order, I realized this man was Eric Garcetti, the president of the council and future mayor of Los Angeles, although we did not know that at the time. There were fifteen council people, seven on each side of Garcetti, and each had their name prominently displayed. Behind the council men were some more people, and I realized one of them was Carmen Trutanich, the city attorney. This was one of the guys who were threatening to raid our stores.

The meeting came to order, and Garcetti called for new business to be discussed. If anyone wanted to address the council, they simply filled out a card and turned it into the security guard who would walk it to the administrator lady up front. I found out from Susan, the hot blonde sitting next to me, that after new business discussions, the medical marijuana discussions would begin. I was pleased to find out Susan was indeed there for the second half of the meeting. I did just happen to mention that I owned a dispensary, which made her eyes light up.

"I'll have to stop by and say hi," she offered. I was hoping she would say that. With that, the meeting continued. Person after person addressed the council and were given two minutes each. Many were talking about zoning or trash pickup schedules, which were not very interesting to me. Once this portion was coming to an end, the last person came up to speak. Surprisingly, he was in a KKK outfit, fully garbed.

Mr. Garcetti asked him to remove his hood, but this man recited a law, I think called Brown's law, which enabled him to remain anonymous at these meetings. So Garcetti finally conceded and said to continue.

Now as the person spoke, it was more than obvious that he was a Black man. His hand protruded from below his white gown, and he spoke with a definite "Black" accent, if there is such a thing. His complaint was that the city of Los Angeles had lost an $800,000 lawsuit to him and still had not paid him. He wanted his money.

Garcetti basically stated that a judge had extended this payment indefinitely because they either had to decide to pay for schools or pay judgments. The judge would always rule on the side of the schools. In other words, they were never going to pay this man.

The man vowed he would not give up the mic until he got paid, and then the real shit show began. One of the Hispanic council members, a man by the name of Tony Cadenas, stood up and, in a really bad attempt at acting, stated, "I'm afraid that a Klan member is here; I cannot stay." Next, Herb Wesson, the only Black councilman, stood up and said the same. One by one, the councilmen filed out of the chamber. Once half of them had left, Garcetti announced, "We no longer have a quorum. Meeting dismissed." And that was that.

Our meeting had just been cancelled. People were visibly upset.

"We need to vote these clowns out of office," one man threatened.

"I guess we are done here today," Susan stated matter-of-factly.

"Are you kidding me? I drove all this way and paid for parking for this?" I complained.

"Well, at least I got to meet you," Susan said. "Are you hiring at the dispensary?"

"Possibly," I said. "You should come down and put in an application."

As she stood up, she grabbed a pair of crutches that had been at her side the whole time. I had assumed they belonged to the person to her right.

"Did you hurt yourself?" I asked.

"Yeah, I blew out my arches at my last job. I'm definitely looking for a desk job as I can't stand without them," she said.

"Well, maybe you could work admin," I told her. "Come down."

"How is tomorrow?" she asked.

"That works. I'll be there all day," I promised.

I walked with her out of the building. At least I had made one new friend. I was still pissed as hell that the council had abandoned their responsibilities. I'm sure they were still planning to collect their paychecks.

On the way down, the man in the white robe was in my elevator and had removed his hood. Sure enough, he was Black. He was apologizing to everyone. He did not mean to end the meeting. He was also showing everyone the judgment.

"It's amazing how the rich and powerful public servants don't have to pay their bills, huh?" I said to him. "Just us little guys."

On the way home I accidentally went down "skid row," which was just packed with homeless people in tents.

"So, this is LA, huh? What a shithole," I thought. This whole council meeting had accomplished nothing but a wasted day. That night on the news, I heard that two Westside dispensaries had been raided. I had also learned this from a few of my new customers, one who had been detained for two hours.

"Yeah, it was horrible," he said. "They walked in in riot gear with guns drawn. Scared the crap out of everyone. The cops were arrogant and bossy. Cuffed the owners and took them out right away. Made one of them open the safe and took out all the money. Then they bagged up all the weed and even removed the flat screen TVs. Anything they could not take, they broke, including the glass display case. These were not cops…they were thugs. It was a shakedown."

Now at that time, I still believed the cops were the good guys and that these dispensaries must have done something to cause this. As time went on, I discovered the real truth. This news highly disturbed me. What would I do if they did the same to me? I had never been arrested in my life. What would my parents think? I decided to eat a couple edibles that night. I hadn't slept well since I first received that letter. Bags were forming under my eyes. Smoking and edibles were my only relief. Oh, and Lorraine. I was on her regular Monday schedule. She would come visit me, and we would smoke out and rape each other for hours on end. She was quite the stress reliever, but sometimes she would disappear for weeks at a time. I just accepted any time she wanted to get together, with no strings attached.

The following week, the dispensary topic had been rescheduled at city council. So, I made my plans to go again, but this time I was pissed. The meeting started at 10:00 a.m. sharp, but this time they went right into the dispensary topic. I met up with Susan in the lobby, and she apologized for not making it to my shop last week. "No big deal. Come down when you can," I told her.

"I can come right after this meeting if you want," she said. "I took the bus here, so I could ride with you if you've got space."

I was incredibly happy I had brought my truck and not my motorcycle that day. I agreed. I'm not known for turning down the company of a beautiful woman.

This time, I filled out a card and wanted to speak. Now I'm about the biggest chicken when it comes to public speaking, but these idiots had really riled me up and I wanted to give them a piece of my mind. Susan had filled out a card as well, and they began calling on people one by one.

Each person that came up was in support of the dispensaries. Only one person was in a neighborhood where she didn't want them. Susan was called next, and she limped up on her crutches. She described the extreme pain she was in and how this drug helped her immensely.

After Susan, my name was called. I was nervous and mad as hell as I approached the podium. Garcetti said, "Welcome," and I thanked him. Then I began to unleash my fury.

"First of all, let me say how very angry I am with all of you walking out on us last week. If you were my employees, I would fire every one of you right on the spot. Perhaps you forgot you are public servants, and you work for us. Second of all, I hear dispensaries are being raided around town. You council members are representatives of the people. We may not agree on everything, but one thing I hope we all agree on is that this is America and we all have rights guaranteed by that flag." I pointed to the flag hanging over the council chambers. "We, the people, are in the process of determining what the laws for medical marijuana should be. Meanwhile you've got this Nazi" (I pointed directly at Carmen Trutanich) "ordering his storm troopers to come kick in our doors and stick guns in our faces for not obeying his orders. Those orders did not come from the people. I would expect this type of treatment in the Soviet Union but not here! Members of the council, I am asking you…no, I'm demanding that you keep your damn dog on a leash," I said as I once again pointed at Trutanich.

Until this point, Trutanich hadn't been paying attention to the meeting, but now he lifted his head and stared right at me. "That's right, sir, I'm talking about you, and you should be listening. That's why we pay you to be here," I said. With that, I stomped away from the microphone and the room went crazy with applause and hoots and hollers.

I walked back to Susan whose eyes were aglow with admiration and a big smile as she joined the clapping. I was hoping this earned me some bedroom brownie points.

"Damn, tell them how you really feel," she said as I sat down. I didn't know it then, but I had just dived face-first into a bowl of piranhas.

As the room calmed down, more speakers came up to the podium, and I sat there coming down off my platitude. It had felt good to give them a piece of my mind. After about a ten-minute period, I was surprised to see one of the councilmen walking down the aisle, seemingly looking for someone. When he saw me, he came over and asked if he could sit down. Surprised, I said sure. He sat there for a second and then began a conversation without actually looking at me. He told me he was Bill Rosendahl and that he was the councilman for my district. He said that, in fact, he only lived about a block from my dispensary. Now Bill was an older, heavyset gentleman. He had a kind face and big hands. When I shook them, his hand engulfed mine.

"I see you came down to make some friends," he said with a laugh. Then in a more serious tone, he said, "You know, Dalton, when they raid you, it destroys your life. They are not nice about it. You need to be careful. You just challenged the city attorney to a fight."

"Well, then mission accomplished," I said. "My kids are raised, and I'm an American patriot fighting for our rights. If I have to go to jail, so be it."

"Honestly, Dalton, I support you guys," he said, "I'm fighting off some cancer myself and just recently lost my life partner."

I found out later that Bill was the first openly gay councilman in the history of LA.

"I wish I could come down and get some product, but it just wouldn't look right," he said.

"Well, Bill, I live at the dispensary, so here is my card and that is my cell phone. If you ever need anything, let me know and I'll deliver it myself,"

With that, he stood up and said, "Keep up the fight."

I smiled and nodded. "Wow, I'm becoming known quickly around here."

Susan said, "Yeah, Bill is awesome. I met him once before at a local district meeting. Nice guy."

At that point, I told Susan I need to hit the bathroom and would be right back. I really was looking for a place to smoke as my excitement level was high and I needed to calm a bit. I noticed there were a set of doorways on the main hall before the council chamber, and many people were walking out them. When I looked out the glass doors, I saw an endless flight of stairs descending three stories to the ground level. I realized that if I went out those doors, I would not be able to reenter, unless I went back around to the main entrance and back through security. Kind of like when you're at an airport and they have no smoking areas past the security gates. I decided to "go for it" because my craving was overwhelming. Then I had an idea. What if I took a business card and jimmied that latch on one of the doors so I could reenter. This would save me from having to go all the way around the building. So that is exactly what I did. Once outside, I sat down on the step and fired up a cigarette. Two minutes later, a building cop came out and started approaching me. "Oh crap," I thought.

"Can I borrow your lighter?" he asked.

"Sure," I said as I handed it to him. He lit up his cigarette, and we engaged in small talk for a couple minutes. As we were standing there, I saw my business card fall out of the door as someone opened the door very quickly.

"Oh well, there goes that plan," I thought. The policeman said "thanks" and then walked down the steps. I stood up and was about ready to follow, when the door swung wide open again and a couple was walking down, talking intensely. Without thinking I made my move and was inside the door before it even came back. I looked around, and there was no one to be seen.

"Hmm, not very secure, was it?" I thought. "Someone with a gun could enter this way very easily."

As I walked toward the chambers, a man with a microphone approached me.

"Wow, that was some statement you made in there," he declared. "Can I get an interview? I'm John Hauffman with the *LA Times*." He gave me a card. He had a cameraman following him as well.

"Ah, sure," I said. "Can I use the restroom first?"

"Take your time," John said. Little did I know I was about to take the national scene.

After using the restroom, I saw that John and his cameraman were all set up on the side of the hallway, and he motioned for me to come over.

"So I'll have you stand right there and just ask you a series of questions," John said. "Which collective do you operate, and where is it located?" he asked.

"I run the Rainforest Collective on Venice Boulevard, in Mar Vista," I responded.

"You're one of the hardship collectives, I take it?" he inquired.

"Yes, we began operations in February of this year," I answered.

"And that's why you are so frustrated with the council today, and, in particular, it seemed you had a problem with the city attorney," he prodded.

"Absolutely, this is ridiculous. We are in a legislative process and instead of the man waiting to see what the people decide, this yahoo is raiding stores and ruining lives," I responded again. The interview went on for several minutes more and then the city council meeting began to let out. Soon, Susan appeared at the door and came over to me, standing right outside of the camera view.

John asked if he could have my phone number for any follow-up questions, and we exchanged cards.

With that, I looked at Susan and asked her if she was ready to go. She said yes, so we joined the stream of people heading toward the elevator. Several other reporters asked me for interviews. One was from a radio station and one from a smaller paper; I obliged. Other people were saying good job to me and giving me high fives. I guess I had said what was on everyone else's minds. As I've said, I wasn't much for public speaking, but now I felt like a champion. What I didn't realize is that I had just poked a sleeping tiger.

Susan and I got down to floor level, and we started walking toward the public parking. I had to walk very slow for her to keep up on her crutches. But honestly, she was so naturally beautiful, I didn't mind the wait. When we got to my truck, I opened the door for her and helped her in the truck. "Always the gentleman," I thought, but I promise you that is not all I was thinking.

"Down boy, down," I said to myself.

As we pushed through the heavy traffic, I found out Susan was from Michigan as well. But she was from the Upper Peninsula, which was about ten hours away from where I grew up.

"Still, those Michigan values and attitudes are always a welcome sight in this big city," I thought.

We talked about the meeting and her thoughts. She said I was very impressive in a very sincere manner. It took us about an hour to get to my shop, and we pulled into the back parking lot. I opened the gate and pulled my vehicle forward, then locked the gate behind us.

"Now you're my prisoner," I stated with a smile.

"Oh no, I'm so scared," she said with her own bit of sexy sarcasm.

As we entered through the back of the shop, we walked right into the dispensary portion. Eric was there working the day shift, and there were two patients there purchasing medicine.

"Hey Eric, been busy?" I inquired.

"Pretty steady," he replied.

"Ring me through," I commanded, meaning let me pass through the man cage. With that, he hit the buzzer that was necklaced around his neck. The lock of the man cage disengaged, and I walked straight through with Susan in tow.

Once we entered the lobby area, April and Passion were up front and greeted me with smiles.

"Hi ladies, this is Susan. She would like an application for a job," I stated. They reached into the file behind them and pulled out an application. We always had a steady stream of applicants. Funny how it seemed everyone and their sister wanted to work at a dispensary. But like they say, it's not what you know but who you know, right?

"Follow me," I instructed Susan as she limped along. Right before the stairway to go up to my apartment, there was a small smoking lounge with a table and a bong (oops, I mean water pipe) sitting on it. The table was surrounded by a sectional couch. I motioned for Susan to sit down and gave her a pen to begin filling out the application.

"Would you like to try some samples?" I asked her, meaning smoke some of the product.

"Well, I'm not going to say no to that," she smiled with appreciation.

"I'll be right back," I promised as I made my way back to the dispensary area of the shop. It was close to five, so the employee shifts were changing to the night crew. Sagi showed up to work the back, and Karen showed up to work the front. As I was getting some samples for Susan, people started piling though the door. I guess the word was out. We were a success. I asked Eric to stay a little longer to help with the rush, which he agreed. The girls up front also agreed to stay longer and I went back to the smoking lounge with samples in hand. From the smoking lounge, I could monitor the entire store, as I had cameras everywhere. Patients were encouraged to stop in the lounge and hang out after their purchase.

"Have you ever smoked from a volcano?" I asked Susan.

"No, I haven't, but I'm willing to try," she said enthusiastically.

Now a volcano is basically a vaporizer with a large plastic bag attached to it. The base is indeed shaped like a volcano and, as the weed is heated, the vapors fill the bag. Once the bag is completely filled, you detach the bag and pass it around to people. They just inhale the invisible vapors, which are very intense. It's like sucking air out of a balloon.

As the bag began to fill, we were joined by a couple of patients and we all began passing around the bag. Susan looked absolutely amazing sitting on my couch conversing with my clients. I thought that with her physical disability, maybe this would be the perfect job for her. Sampling weed with our clients. Not a bad job, I thought, and damn that would bring them back for more.

As the night continued, it started dying down around 8:00 p.m., and Eric asked if he could get off, which I allowed. April soon popped her head in and asked the same thing and I said "fine."

Both April and Eric joined us in the lounge. Now as a policy at the end of every shift, my employees received a free gram of pot in addition to their pay. This policy served two purposes really. First of all, how can they recommend a strain if they haven't smoked it? Second of all, if I was giving them weed, perhaps they wouldn't steal from me. I had made it very clear from the beginning that if anyone stole from me, they would be prosecuted to the fullest extent of the law.

"Are you going to hire some more people?" asked Amy, never shy to confront a situation. "We have been getting hella busy lately."

"I'm glad you asked that," I responded. "The answer is yes. In fact, I just hired one of my old high school friends from Michigan, and he will be driving out next week."

I realized that the legal battle was going to take a lot of my time, so I needed to get a manager in to constantly be there when I was not.

Skip and I had first met when we were twelve or thirteen, back in Boy Scouts. As we got older and went into high school, Skip began to have a crush on my younger sister Tammy. Skip had always been a good sidekick and when I joined the wrestling team, he joined also. Skip was quite a bit larger than I was, but I was a much more skilled wrestler and I also hit the weights a lot more often, so he always remained a sidekick. He and my sister dated for the last two years of high school until she went off to college and he went into the Navy.

I needed someone I trusted so I tracked him down back in my old hometown and offered him a job at $60,000 per year. He jumped at the opportunity. He was supposed to arrive the next week.

Closing time was 10:00 p.m. during the week so soon the remaining employees Marco, Sagi, and Brittany were filing into the smoking lounge. We escorted our final client out the door, and it was just me and the crew. We smoked out for a while and then I invited everyone over to the Good Hurt for drinks. We all walked as a group a block up the street and made our way into the bar. I noticed Eric and April were holding hands, so my hunch about "office romance" had come true.

To be honest, I was hoping something might happen between myself and Susan that night.

The bar was rocking with a local band, and we all went out on the Daltonce floor, including Susan with her crutches. We were actually "living the life," as so many people say. Yes, indeed; life was good.

As we sat down at the table, we were greeted by the usual staff. Marilyn Monroe was working behind the bar, and we had our normal waitress, who always gave us great service. Jason peeked his head out of the back to say "hi" as usual and promised we must get together soon.

"I guess that's just what people say in LA," I thought.

We were never getting together…I was sure by now.

Sagi and Marco scoured the audience, looking for single, unsuspecting females, and Susan and I sat really close together. I used the loud music from the band as an excuse to get even closer.

"So tell me, how was your first day of work?" I asked, hoping for a positive response.

"You call that work?" she responded. "Sitting around smoking bowls with clients? That's my kind of job, for sure. That was awesome," she said.

"Well, you sure looked damn good sitting on my couch and I could tell all of the male clients enjoyed your company," I told her with a smile.

"Making men happy, that's job number one," she said.

"Oh really, I like that attitude," I said with even more interest. "Now you said you had a 'shoot' tomorrow? What's that all about?"

"Yeah, we are shooting some scenes tomorrow," she affirmed.

"Now how does that work?" I asked her in earnest. "How can you shoot a scene if you can't walk?"

"Well, the scene we are shooting tomorrow, I won't need to walk. I'm just sitting at a bar stool," she explained.

"Oh OK, well that works for tomorrow, I guess, but how about the other days? Sooner or later, you've got to get up off that bar stool. Right?" I asked her, even more confused. At that point, she took me by the hand and looked me deep in the eyes. I forgot how pretty her blue eyes were.

"Dalton, can I tell you something and you won't think bad of me?" she asked.

"Ah sure," I said, now totally confused.

"Well, Dalton. The movie I'm making tomorrow is kind of…a porn movie. Well, I mean, not kind of. It *is* a porn movie, so no, I don't ever have to stand up." She laughed at her quick-witted joke. "Do you hate me now?"

"No, but I am a little shocked," I admitted. You see, coming from another part of the country with conservative values, I had never met a porn star before. "Um…Wow. That's all I can say to that."

I think we were both embarrassed. All of a sudden, conversation was awkward. I had a million questions in my head but wasn't sure if any were appropriate.

"So, do you make good money?" I asked, staying on the business end of things.

"Sometimes," she said. "I'm getting $500 tomorrow; sometimes I get $1,000."

"Well, you got to do what you got to do to pay the bills," I said. "You just caught me a little off guard as I saw you as this little wholesome girl from Michigan," I said, trying to justify my reaction. "I've just never known someone who did that for a living," I said.

"But I'm sure you've watched a lot of them, huh?" she asked with a smile.

"Well, I don't know about a lot, but I definitely want to see this one…" I teased.

"Why watch when you can participate?" she flirted as she reached under the table and grabbed my leg.

"No reason I can think of," I came back with.

"Wow! Am I really gonna make it with a porn star tonight?" I thought to myself. I was both nervous and extremely excited. "I love LA. I *love* LA."

The night started winding down and one by one, the employees said their goodbyes, until it was just me and Susan sitting at the bar. We were both way beyond intoxicated at this point.

"Well, I'm sorry to tell you, young lady, but I'm way too drunk to drive you home, so you are either staying at my house or I'm calling you a cab," I stated.

"We can go back to your place," she said. As we both stumbled off our stools, the owner Justin came out to say his goodbyes as we made our way to the door.

"We need to get together soon," he repeated.

"Just call me," I responded as we walked out into the cool summer air. I tried to help Susan as best I could as we walked back to the dispensary. When we went in, I asked her if she wanted to smoke out some more and she did, so I grabbed the volcano and said, "Let's take this upstairs."

We both barely made it to the top of the stairs and plunked down on the couches. Susan laid back on the couch and kicked off her shoes. She looked damn good on my couch, I thought. This is going to be fun.

"I've got to use the restroom," I said.

She didn't even acknowledge my words.

When I got back from the restroom, she had rolled over and was fast asleep. At first, I was hellbent on taking this fantasy off my bucket list, but every attempt to revive Susan failed.

"Sleep doesn't sound half bad," I thought so I went to my room and was out before I hit the mattress.

At about 7:00 a.m., I awoke with an extreme woody. Visons of Susan had Daltonced in my head all night, and then I remembered this bombshell was out sleeping on my couch. Now it was time to fulfill my destiny… Perhaps…maybe…

When I came out to the couch, it was empty. My body was all revved up with nowhere to go.

"Oh well," I thought. "I'll see her again, I'm sure. For now, I guess I'll have to take care of myself in the shower. I hoped Susan was only half as good as my imagination was conjuring up in that hot, steamy shower. I would really let her have it.

Chapter 11: The Eyes of a Nation
The next day was cold and rainy.

The summer was upon us and, I'll tell you, I was quite surprised. You always hear about sunny California, but most days were rainy and overcast. At about 11:00 a.m., a postal worker entered the store and gave me another certified letter in the mail, this time from the city council. They were scheduling hardship review meetings for each dispensary, and mine was scheduled for July 8. The council had instructed the district attorney to allow them to handle the matter and to stop the raids until they had this review. This caused a lot of friction between the council and the attorney office. They did not like to be told what to do.

At noon, I received a call, which April handed over to me. It was the *Wall Street Journal* asking for an interview. I guess they had read the *LA Times* piece and wanted to come down to my store for an interview. I said, "Sure," and we made arrangements for the following Monday. My phone was making some weird clicking sounds, and I chalked it up to a bad connection.

Later in the afternoon I got on my cell phone to call Skip and get an update. He said he would definitely be here by Monday also. I told him about the *Wall Street Journal* coming and about all the other events that had transpired since last we talked. I sure was glad to be getting my old sidekick back. The clicking on my cell phone mimicked the clicking I had heard on the store phone. How odd, I thought.

A little while later, Susan called and apologized for skipping out so early. I guess she was having a photo shoot or an audition or something up north and needed to get home and get ready. Click, click, click, the phone continued.

At about 5:30 p.m., I was sitting in the lounge, talking to a vendor, when Karen entered the lounge and asked for my assistance. She brought me out to the front desk and there was a fifty-something gentleman sitting there in a polo shirt and khakis.

"Now Dalton, I'm really confused, but when I run this gentleman's medical card, it keeps coming us as owned by a nineteen-year-old girl named Sasha," Karen explained.

"Hmm…Must be a glitch in the system," I said as I verified this information. "Sure enough," I said as the man shrugged and gave me a confused look.

"Can I just pick up a small amount?" he asked, with a little pity in his voice, but just then something struck me wrong. Something about his mannerisms did not add up.

"Let me go back and check something," I told the man as I walked back to the lounge. I really just went there to gather my thoughts. I remembered hearing a story of how the police were sending in undercover officers to see if they could buy with an invalid ID. Once successful, they would get a judge's order to raid the place within the week. I had a sneaking suspicion that's what this was.

I walked back out to the gentleman and asked if he had any additional ID. He shook his head and then turned his body to block my view of his wallet. He wasn't able to show me any other ID.

"Well, sir, I am truly sorry, but we must abide by the law in every circumstance. Go get your MJ card fixed and then I can serve you."

"OK," he said as he grabbed his things and high-tailed it out of there. I gathered my employees and told them that this was an attempt by an undercover cop to enter our building. I told everyone that they needed to always make 1,000 percent sure that these people were valid before selling them anything. They all agreed. I was shaking with a combination of fear and anger. This was my government trying to set me up.

"Don't they have real criminals to catch?" I wondered.

Then I started thinking about the clicking sounds I had been hearing. Was I being taped? I wondered if all the weed I had been smoking lately was making me paranoid. Then I remembered a favorite saying of mine: "Just because you are paranoid doesn't mean someone is *not* trying to kill you."

At about 7:00 p.m., I got a call from Donald Smith, the airline pilot and silent partner. He was just calling to check up on sales and things. Again, the click, click, click continued.

"Hold on, David," I said. Then I said, "I can tell that I am being taped by federal agents. I am not doing anything to break the law and if the rumors are true, you are raiding and robbing people all across the city and not claiming everything you take. You deserve the punishment you will get," I threatened.

And then, wow, I heard the distinct sound of a tape being rewound. As if it was being erased. Then the clicking sound stopped and the phone was as clear as day.

"Hey David, sorry about that. It seems I'm being taped by federal agents. For what, I do not know."

David understandably wanted to keep the conversation short. I agreed. I guess someone had read my comments to the *LA Times* and wanted to shut me down. We will see, I thought. I don't scare easily...

Or so I thought. I decided to call it an early night, went to the lounge, smoked a bowl, and ate an edible, then hit the sack. The employees could handle things. I was floating on cloud nine.

* * *

It was pitch black in my apartment as the apartment had no windows. I was awoken abruptly by a huge bang coming from the downstairs lobby. I turned on the light in my bedroom and heard several voices downstairs. They were saying, "Go, go, go," and "This is the police. Everyone lay down on the ground with your hands behind your head."

I ran to the top of the stairway and looked down. There was a guy in black riot gear standing over two of my employees, who were laying half-dressed on the couch. I recognized them as April and Eric. I thought this was odd because why would they still be here? They had gotten off work at 5:00 p.m. Eric was just staring at me with a weird grin, and April was cleaning the table as the man had his gun steadied on them. I could hear a bunch of commotion in the dispensary area, including the breaking of glass.

I heard one man say, "What do we do with the TVs?"

Another cop answered, "Take them. My son needs a new one for his room." And they both laughed.

Then I heard a voice come from behind me. It was Skip.

"Oh man, you scared me," I said, "When did you get here?"

"Dalton, this isn't real," Skip said. "Dude you're just tripping."

It took me a minute to understand and then I realized that what he was saying was true. I forced myself to wake up out of the deep sleep I was in. My dreams had become so real. I was sweating bullets but was glad this was only a dream…this time. This time. Every night, I was finding it harder and harder to sleep. It was easy to put out of my mind when I was awake but when my subconscious took over, then damn. I was at the mercy of my fears. I needed to find a refuge. Sleeping in the dispensary wasn't good because I was beginning to be paranoid all the time.

"Once Skip gets here, I need to take a little vacation," I thought. With that, I tried to make it through the rest of the night.

The weekend was very busy, so I stayed to help out. Susan had started her shifts from five to ten, just hanging out in the lounge with our guests. I bought a trivia card game for her to interact with the guests and keep them interested. After the first night, however, we had to put an hour limit for all guests because some wanted to just stay all night for the free samples. I went back behind the counters to help them during the rush and little Brittany was back there. I'll tell you, it was extremely hard to focus with her little butt crack protruding from her little shorts all night, but I made it. Marco and Joshua were also working, and I kind of noticed a kind of arrogance in Joshua, like he was way too knowledgeable for this place. Marco was great with the customers and had some good rapport. The night ended well, with record sales.

June 2009

Monday came soon enough, and I got a call from Skip that he was about four hours away. I told him he had forgotten how bad LA traffic was, so I gave him eight hours.

Lorraine texted me and told me she would be stopping by for our Monday night romp. God, I loved that girl. Just here to have fun and score some free pot. Win-win, I say.

At about 9:00 p.m., Skip texted me that he was outside the shop. I made Lorraine get dressed as I went down to meet him. I met him at the front door, and we gave each other a warm hug. I hadn't seen Skip in years.

Despite the fact that he was two years my junior, his hair had become prematurely white. I actually could only recognize him by his eyes.

"You were right about the eight hours," he said. "Where should I park?"

"Drive around back," I said. "I'll meet you back there."

I walked back through the man cage and through the dispensary to the back doors, opened them, and walked to the chain link fence. I had the padlock undone by the time Skip pulled around the corner.

I waved him in and was happy to see he had only a small car. He fit in perfectly.

"Grab your bags," I said as I locked up the gates and grabbed a small bag he had set out on the pavement.

We walked back through the dispensary, through the cage, and into the lounge where Lorraine had made her way down and was talking to a guest while smoking out.

I introduced Skip as we walked up the stairs. As soon as we entered the apartment and closed the door, he said, "Damn, who was that girl on the couch?"

"Hands off," I said. "She's mine."

"You dog, same as always," he said. "You've always had hot girlfriends."

"This is your room, and here's the bathroom," I said. "Do you need to take a shower or anything?"

"A shower would be awesome," he said.

"Here's a towel. Make yourself at home," I said as I gave him a towel. "Come down to join us whenever you're ready or crash, whatever you like."

"Yeah, I need to crash," he said.

"So be it. See you tomorrow, then." With that, I left him.

As I came back down the stairs, I noticed Lorraine was gathering a fan club. The guys were all hanging out trying to talk to her.

"What an advantage women have," I thought. "They don't even have to say a damn thing; just smile."

"Let's go," I commanded. She jumped up and followed dutifully. I must say I was a little jealous of all the male attention she was getting.

We walked down to the Good Hurt and ordered some burgers and beers and sat there eating, drinking, and kissing the rest of the night. My kind of girl, I thought. After dinner, we went back to my room and used and abused each other for several more hours. Lorraine always snuck out before any employees arrived. She called it the walk of shame. I sure as hell wasn't ashamed of tagging that, however.

It was now Tuesday, the big day. *The Wall Street Journal* was supposed to arrive at 9:00 a.m. They called at about 8:30 a.m. and arrived about fifteen minutes later. They wanted to do a whole story with photos and all. Now, to be honest, I had no idea what a can of worms I was opening by inviting them in. You see, I was the first person to ever allow cameras into a working dispensary.

"Why?" you ask. Well, think about it.

I was allowing them to film me *breaking federal law*. In other words, I was committing a felony in front of the cameras. But, as I have said before, I am an American patriot and I believe freedom isn't free. I believed that the people of the state of California had decided something, and I was here to enforce it.

I believed that if the people wanted the government to paint the street purple, it's the government's job to ask, "What shade?" Somewhere along the line, the government had seized way too much power, and it was my job to turn the table back in the right direction. I was either brave or stupid. Probably the latter.

They showed up with just two people, and one was carrying the camera. We sat in the smoking lounge, and they asked tons and tons of questions. They were trying to probe and pry to find out how much money I was making. To be honest, I hadn't even had time to calculate that, because when you start a new business, you always have more money going out than coming in.

They asked me to show them the product, so I took them back to the dispensary and showed them everything. They asked me to weigh some pot on the scale, and that was the shot that made the journal. I gave them everything they needed and more. Two days later, there was a full page about me in the journal. I was now the face of medical marijuana in Los Angeles.

After that, I was constantly being hounded for interviews. Every time Stephen Cooley or Trutanich made a statement about shutting us down, the papers and TV networks called me to get the rebuttal. I was getting equal time with the district and city attorneys of Los Angeles.

My dad called me on the phone and told me how proud he was that I was bucking the system. Our business doubled, and we became famous around LA.

Chapter 12: Hardship Review
July 2009

J uly 8 was coming up soon, so it was time to start preparing for it. I decided to give David Welch a call and see if he wanted to accompany me. He agreed.

When the day came, we met at the City Hall building near the front door. We went through security and made our way to the elevators. Out review was scheduled for 11:00 a.m. and was only to last half an hour. I had probably smoked half a pack of cigarettes that morning and drunk half a pot of coffee, so to say I was jittery was an understatement.

There were ten dispensaries on the docket for review that day, and, fortunately, we were number two. We stayed outside the room, and David went over the script of what to say and not to say. You see, this meeting was for us to justify our hardship. Our justification was, and it was bogus, that because federal agents had been raiding stores and not honoring the legal dispensaries, that we were in fear of opening or even applying. Fear of arrest was our hardship. A totally valid argument.

Soon, it became our turn to enter the chamber room. At a large, long desk, there were three council members. To the far right was a man named Jose Huizar. He was a large, Hispanic man with a stern look and a pock-marked face. He barely even acknowledged the fact we had entered the room. I could tell from the energy he put off that he was an arrogant, self-serving, piece of shit. In the middle was a man named Dennis

Zine, who was a retired police chief sucking up more government payroll. Knowing that he came from the LAPD already told me everything I needed to know about this guy. Corrupt to the core. The third man on the left, however, had a completely different energy about him. His name was Ed Reyes, and he was the one spearheading the effort to bring the "scourge" of dispensaries under control. I could tell he was doing his job in earnest without ulterior motives. A true servant of the people.

Mr. Reyes began the review by having me state my name, the name and address of my dispensary, and the reason for my hardship. Mr. Welch then introduced himself as my attorney and outlined in legal terms why my hardship was indeed valid.

As Mr. Reyes reviewed my documents, Mr. Huizar made some rude comments about how we were all out just to make a bunch of cash and didn't really care about our patients' wellbeing. Zine basically stated these dispensaries were disrupting neighborhoods, and they needed to be closed down to a reasonable number.

Then, Mr. Reyes pulled a note out of my file.

"Now, wait a minute here," Mr. Reyes said. "There is a note from the Councilman Rosendahl for his district. Mr. Rosendahl supports this dispensary remaining open. I think we should adjourn until we can consult Mr. Rosendahl," Reyes declared.

Jose Huizar stepped in. "I say we just take a vote now," he said with his overbearing arrogance.

Mr. Reyes complied. "Mr. Huizar, do you support this hardship, yea or nay?"

"Nay," said Huizar.

"Mr. Zine?"

"Nay."

Reyes reluctantly voted nay also.

"The nays have it. You hardship is not approved. This order will not take effect until approved by the General Council."

And that was that. A week later, I received the certified document of our denial.

Over the next few weeks, all hardships were denied. It was like the Salem witch trials—no chance of reprieve.

August 2009

At this point, I had two choices. Accept this ruling or declare war on this corrupt political machine. Who were they to tell the people what we could and could not do? My business was doing well now, and I thought it was time to get organized and prepare for a fight.

I appointed one of my staff members, Cindy, nicknamed by the other staffers "Tits McGee" because of how she loved to display her fine rack, to be the leader of my organization's movement.

My plan was to form a political nonprofit group and pull all the dispensaries together to act as one unit rather than be picked off one at a time. What I had discovered in the last few weeks is that the established dispensaries that had been around before the moratorium were actually working with the city to eradicate the rest of us. There were seventy of them and hundreds of us. Of course, it was in their best interest to eliminate the competition, but I knew that if the hardship dispensaries combined forces, we could outpower all of them.

Thus, the Green Alliance of Patients and Providers (GAPP) was born. Quickly, Cindy and I recruited a group of "salespeople" to go out to each dispensary in our situation and invite them to a meeting. Mark and I would run the meeting, and we also invited David Welch to speak.

We set the meeting for two weeks out and went to work. The meeting was held on a Monday night. Over eighty dispensaries were in attendance. My whole lobby was full, and it came to standing room only.

I was the first to speak. I introduced myself and told them of my plans. Now I had already gained a lot of street credit from the *Wall Street Journal* ad and from my outburst at City Hall, so everyone treated me with a bit of reverence. I told them that the city had been pushing us around too much, and it was time to start pushing back. I could feel the energy in the room building and building. One thing that became very clear to me as I spoke to this crowd was that I was the minority.

Of the eighty-some people in the room, most were Hispanic or Arabic, surprisingly. Some were Jewish. Some were Africans from Africa. I felt like Attila the Hun trying to rally a group of barbarians to take on the legions of Rome. But like Attila, I thought we could win the day. I was greeted with cheers of approval.

Next Mark spoke. Remember, they all knew him because he had gotten their hardship application approved originally. He spoke to the faulty reasoning behind the government's actions.

Then David Welch spoke and told them the course of action that he thought was most likely to succeed.

You see, they had just cancelled the hardship extension, but the moratorium had been illegally extended last time and was due to expire again. It had put in place as an emergency measure, over two years ago. In other words, if we attack the moratorium, we don't need the hardships. Brilliant!

By the end of the evening, the mission was accomplished. The GAPP was formed, and officers were appointed. Now we were ready for battle.

September to October 2009

Right on schedule, the moratorium was defeated, and it became the Wild West all over again, with new dispensaries opening daily. The city council got caught with their pants down and began scrambling to get some type of ordinance to curb the growth.

In October of 2009, the city set up a debate at City Hall to hear both side of the debate. Four hundred advocates showed up, including forty or so GAPP members. Only four opponents showed up. When I went up to speak, my whole group cheered and I felt like a somebody as I approached the podium. By the end of the meeting, the council members looked visibly exhausted. They were outnumbered and outsmarted. I really thought they had cracked and given in. We all walked out of there feeling we had won the day. Let freedom ring.

Despite the huge public outcry to just leave the dispensaries alone, I saw myself on a news channel that night. The fake news media made it seem like I was an outraged citizen and wanted the stores closed. This was my first experience with fake news, long before Trump named it.

By December, the city council had hustled though an ill-conceived ordinance, using zoning, to pretty much ban all dispensaries. They were sick of the debate and were trying to end it once and for all.

They called another chamber meeting for public input and then limited us to only fifteen seconds. It was obvious they did not care about our input. I used my fifteen seconds to threaten them with the impending legal action we planned as well as to mention pulling Jose Huizar out of his set. Everyone knew what a low-life criminal he was, even back then. Rumor had it he and his buddy Villarosa were profiting heavily from the illegal drug trafficking in Los Angeles.

During this time, the LAPD, along with federal agents, decided it was a good time to step up raids, using "the public good" as an excuse to exercise Nazi tactics against their own citizens. You see, what I had learned over the last few months was how truly horrific and dishonest these raids were. I was also warned that I was being targeted and that I really needed to be careful.

One of my vendors had been out at a shop—a pot shop. When he walked to the back, there were four uniformed police officers back there. They were not there to close the place but in fact were running the place. It became well known throughout our ranks that when police raided our stores, they stole everything of value. They even went to the store own-ers' houses and took guns, money, televisions, cars, and whatever else they wanted. Then the marijuana was taken to one of the "police-run dispen-saries" and sold. They also did this with normal drug busts of street drugs. In other words, the LAPD, combined with federal agents, were running a *cartel* and a money laundering operation and members of the city coun-cil knew about it. As an American patriot, I was shocked by what I had learned.

The phone recordings continued. On one particular call, a good friend of mine in Colorado, by the name of Jake, had suggested I run a truckload of weed up to Denver. He said that we could make a shit-ton of cash. Immediately, I jumped in to correct him. My standard telephone conver-sation went exactly like this:

"Hey Jake, just to let you know, but we are being taped by federal agents right now." Click, click, click. "And to the federal agents that are on the line, I have a message for you. I'm aware of your money launder-ing activities. I know where your stores are located. You are wearing an American badge and fighting on the side of the cartels, which makes you a traitor to this country, and you will receive a traitor's fate. You are robbing and raiding our dispensaries and reselling the goods in your own stores. I have all the evidence against you and if anything happens to me, if I get arrested or end up dead in some freak accident, I want you to know one thing. This information is housed in seven different offices here in the city of LA and in other states. Once my attorneys get news of my arrest or demise, they are instructed to send this information to my contacts at the *Wall Street Journal* and the associated press for distribution. You are a disgrace to your uniform."

With that statement, I would hear the familiar sound of tapes being rewound and erased. You see, these dirty police—the DEA, the FBI, and the LAPD—could not use these tapes in court without now prompting an investigation.

I also hired a private investigator to start poking around the stores that I knew were police "front shops."

I was playing a high-risk game of poker with federal agents and the city of LA. Not only did I have to worry about the cartels coming after me; I had to worry about the cops also. I felt like I was living in a third-world country.

I'll be honest, the stress was getting to me. If you look at the online videos and photos of me over this time, I started gaining a lot of weight. I went from a size 32 pants to a size 40 in about a year. My blood pressure was through the roof, and I hadn't slept well in weeks.

I decided I needed to take a little vacation for a few days, and what better place than Tijuana, Mexico. The next morning, I headed down and was at the border by noon. Crossing the border was noneventful, and I jumped in a car.

"Adelita Bar, please," I commanded as I eased back and relaxed.

It might sound strange, but all of a sudden, I felt more comfortable in Mexico than I did in my own country. I realized I could sleep soundly without the fear of Gestapo-like police storming my room. I arrived at Adelita's very quickly and tipped my driver and the doorman. As I slid through the red curtain, the familiar sights and sounds took over. I sat at the bar and ordered a Pacífico. I planned to spend a couple days here, so I went up to the hotel and reserved a room. This way, if I met a girl, I didn't have to pay an hourly rate.

There were about twenty girls in Adelita's, and it was kind of dead, so I decided to walk down the road about half a block to a bar called Hong Kong. Now Hong Kong always had a lot more action going on, even during the day. The girls were all required to be dancing whenever guests were in the bar and the bar was open twenty-four seven. As I walked in, the security guard welcomed me. It seemed he remembered me from last time. He wanded me quickly, then said, "Paseo," so I passed.

Girls were dancing on every bar, and I grabbed a seat in the middle, so I had a good view of all the action.

As soon as the girls saw me come in, they began to dive bomb me with propositions of going upstairs. I always guarded my seat so they could not invite themselves to sit down. I liked to spend the first hour getting my beer goggles on and playing hard to get. It was a very competitive environment for the girls.

I watched the center stage as the performers amazed me with their acrobatics on the pole and the rings. These girls were no joke. Young, firm, and strong. I ventured over to the stage to drop off a few dollars to one amazingly stunning blond performer and she bent down, kissed me on the cheek, and offered to come to my table. She was by far the most popular dancer and had at least a hundred bills on the floor, but these girls preferred Americans over the locals. It wasn't just about the money. It was the fact that we were gentlemen. "Caballeros," as they called us in Spanish. Once she completed another dance, she made her way off stage and eyed me to see if I still wanted company. I definitely did. She walked over to me, topless in her high heels. Her hair was platinum blond, and her makeup was done exquisitely. Now I think when people think of Mexican women, they don't think of blondes, but this is because not many of them cross the border. Over Mexico's history, there has been much German and Russian influence, especially in certain areas of Mexico. Guadalajara, in particular, is home to the most beautiful women in Mexico, many with blond hair and blue eyes. That's where "Barbie" was from.

She was definitely a high-end girl. She was accompanied by a waiter who quickly asked if I wanted to buy "Barbie" a drink.

I did, so he handed me Barbie's hand, and she had a seat on my lap. She was firm but sweaty. I liked that.

We both ordered a beer. Mine was a full-sized beer, and they gave her a much smaller one. Mine cost $4, and hers was $7. With each drink I purchased for her, she received another ticket. It was the goal of each girl to gather 30 tickets over the course of their shift, or they would have to pay for the tickets themselves. Kind of the cost of doing business, I guess.

We finished our first drinks, and I asked her if she would do a shot with me, which she agreed to. Two more beers and two more shots later, we were both feeling kind of good. She asked me if I was ready to go upstairs, but, to be honest, I was just enjoying being here, with her, in Mexico. So I wasn't in a rush.

"No ahora," I responded. "Pero pronto," I said looking at her generous breasts and perfect body.

With that, she said something to the waiter and he moved us to a more private table, out of the center of the room. There, she started touching me and kissing me. Allowing me to touch her wherever I wanted. After a few minutes of this, she had me.

"Arriba?" she asked again.

"Sí," I responded. She called the waiter, who emptied our drinks into plastic cups and walked behind her to the door. Her body was perfect from all angles, with not a hint of cellulose. We got to the front door and the same security guard looked at me and congratulated me on my choice of girls. He dressed her in a robe, then stuck out his hand for a tip. I gave him a five, and he opened the door for us to go to the hotel upstairs. Same routine at the front counter. Except this time, I didn't need to pay for the room.

We got to the fifth floor, and Barbie took my key and led the way.

We opened the room and walked in. Barbie slammed the door behind us. We both eagerly ripped off each other's clothes, and she removed her heels. When she stood back up, she had lost a good four inches of height. She must have been about five foot four, I thought.

I picked her up and carried her to the bed and started licking and caressing her beautiful natural breasts. She rolled me over and started giving me oral with no condom. I laid back and watched as her beautiful neck and body bobbed in unison. The whole time, her eyes stared directly into mine. This was like a scene from a movie. This girl was incredible, and if I had to bet money, I would say she was more excited than I was. She was trying to make a statement.

As she slowly climbed up my body until we were face to face, she said, "No otra mujeres" as she began deep kissing me. She was telling me I could not be with any other women. She was claiming me. Then she slid herself on top of me and started sliding up and down. She was very moist and surprisingly tight. Then I realized she had never put a condom on, so I pushed her back and asked, "No condom?"

"Es problema?" she asked. I was so far in her trance at that point that I said, "No problema" and we continued our mutual molestation of each other savagely. We must have gone for a good hour before we both collapsed from exhaustion.

"Wow," is all I could say. I stared at her hot, sweaty, perfect body as we both laid there in disbelief. Had we had really connected or was she just a great actor, I wondered?

It didn't really matter to me. It was hot and very stress relieving. That's what I had come for. After another twenty minutes, she asked if I was coming back down with her. I opted to stay in my room and take a nap. So she slid back into her tiny outfit and made her way to the door. I went to give her money, but she stopped me.

"You don't pay," she said. Then she reminded me, "No otra mujeres." I soon learned that this was a code with a girl like this. It meant she really liked me so she would not charge me and she didn't wear a condom, which meant I was now her boyfriend and I was not allowed to be with other women. Those were the rules, I guess. Well, I could live with that, I guess.

"She's stunning. Why would I want another woman?" I though naively.

I fell asleep totally in love with this whole new world I had discovered. Here I was, an overweight, forty-five-year-old man kicking it with a model in another country. "Wow, life is good."

I slept for hours. When I awoke, it was extremely dark outside. I had no clue what time it was, and my phone had run out of charge. My mouth was dry, and I needed water badly. Of course, we have all heard the warnings about not drinking the water, so I needed to work my way back to the bar. I walked back down to the dance club and was greeted by a different security guard. There was a short line to get in, and this time they were charging a cover of five dollars. "No problem," I thought as I walked in.

The bar was much, much busier at this time. I asked a waiter and he informed me it was after midnight. The crowd was mainly Mexican, and there was only one seat at the bar, so I grabbed it. Right in front of my seat, a dancer stood at on the bar. She was dressed in a Catholic schoolgirl outfit and had on long Bobby socks. As I sat down, she gave me a nice smile and bent down to kiss me on the cheek. I tipped her a dollar for the kind gesture. I could tell this girl was sweet. She was quite petite also. I didn't imagine she weighed much more than 90 lb. Her long, dark hair was perfectly straight and reached all the way down below her ass. She started Dancing for me on the bar and I gave her another dollar. Then her expression changed as she looked over my shoulder. I turned to see Barbie standing right behind me. "No otra mujeres," she reminded me as she took my hand and pulled me away from the bar.

She took me to an upstairs balcony area, and we sat at a booth. Along the way, she had invited a couple of her girlfriends to join us, so there were three ladies at my table. She called the waiter over and ordered food and drinks for all the people at the table. The food and drinks came and each lady received her ticket. Barbie sat at my side and massaged my inner thigh, touching me to see if she could get me hard again. She was successful. Just then, she got a call for her to dance, so she gave me her purse and told me to wait there. The two girls remained with me and as she left, she pointed and said, "Recuerdo." She was reminding me of the rules again.

Her dance was amazing, and she got a standing ovation. It was clear every guy wanted to take her upstairs, but she came back to me. I guess the rule was, as long as I was in the room, there were no other guys also.

I paid the tab, and we went back to my room for round two. When she had totally worn me out again, she left me and I faded back to sleep. She promised she would return. I awoke the next morning alone. I took this as my opportunity to check out of the hotel and move down to another hotel close by. As much as I enjoyed the previous night, I definitely was not looking for a monogamous relationship with a stripper, as fun as that sounds. I decided I could not return back to Hong Kong on this trip and would let things cool with my newfound girlfriend.

The next night was interesting. I was still nursing a hangover from the night before, so I kind of laid low for most of the day. At about dinner time, I ventured out for tacos and there was a stand located on the corner that was reputed to have the best street tacos in Mexico. I went over and wolfed a couple down. I will tell you, they were and still are the best tacos I have ever had.

I peeked my head into Adelitas and grabbed a beer. It was a Saturday, and it was just starting to get a little busy. I decided to walk down to another bar I knew, where I had met a waiter who had helped me score a joint. Usually, the best medicine for a hangover was a joint, I had discovered.

When I walked into the bar, I saw my friend Julio, who greeted me at the door.

"Bienvenido, Dalton," he said with a smile. "What can I get you to drink?"

"I'll take a beer and a shot," I decided.

"Would you like the company of one of our ladies?" he asked as he pointed to a table with four young girls. They immediately got up and started walking toward my table.

"Not right now," I told him. He disappointedly waved the girls off. One of them made her way to the stripping pole in the middle of the room. I guess she thought I needed a little convincing. I'm not gonna lie, she looked damn good, but I wasn't there for this, so I doubted I could be tempted. I was out of bullets.

Julio returned with the drinks. They were having a two-for-one special on Te Cate, so I opted in. He also brought me my shot.

"You sure you don't want a lady?" he offered again. "This one is very nice." He pointed at the one dancing.

"She is, Julio, but, to be honest, I was hoping you could hook me up with a joint like last time."

"I really don't have any," he said but told me he could look around. He was obviously disappointed that I was here for that and not for the ladies.

"Could you, Julio?" I asked. "Then maybe I'll come back later for the ladies." I think both of us knew that was not true.

"I'll check for you," he promised. He went to take to the bartender, then to the front door guy. Then he walked out to the street. I waited for almost an hour until he finally returned. I had no idea he would take that long. It had already gotten dark outside. I was impatient to get going.

"How much do I owe you, Julio?" I asked.

The bill was less than twenty dollars and I gave him another twenty for the joint.

"Are we good?" I asked him. He barely made eye contact. He was mad. "Yeah, go," he said.

All of a sudden, I didn't feel good about this whole situation. Where had he been for almost an hour? Why was he so upset with me? It was not a good idea to get caught with drugs in Mexico. We have all heard horror stories about that.

"I should use the bathroom first," I announced as I stood up and walked past the table of ladies. I felt like everyone was staring at me. Something didn't feel right. When I got in the stall, my first instinct was to flush the joint down the toilet. Better safe than sorry, right? Risk versus reward? But the risk-taker side kicked in, and I thought how great it would be to be high in Adelita's tonight. Now I had been searched by Mexican police before, and the one thing I always noticed is they never asked you to remove your shoes. They emptied out your pockets and frisked your genital area but never removed the shoes.

I sat down on the edge of the toilet and removed my left shoe and sock. I took the joint and curled it underneath my toes and replaced the sock. I slipped my shoe back on and walked out the door of the bathroom. Julio was standing at the bar and said, "Goodbye amigo" with very little enthusiasm.

I walked out into the night air and made my way to the corner. I was probably just being paranoid but, hey, it was no joke to get busted with weed in Mexico.

As I began to cross the street, a Federali pickup truck approached me with its high beam headlamps focused right on me. I tried to walk around, but he parked in the middle of the road and the passenger door opened up and a young officer jumped out.

"Amigo," he said. "Come here." I still wasn't sure he was talking to me, but then the officer approached and instructed me to follow him to the curb. The other officer parked the truck and exited the vehicle.

"What are you doing here, amigo?" he asked.

"I am a tourist on vacation," I said in broken Spanish with a fake bewildered look on my face. I knew what was up. The waiter had set me up. That prick. He was pissed that I didn't want his girls.

"Do you mind if we search you, amigo?" the driver said.

"Not at all," I said, a little nervous but honestly a little more defiant as I knew who would win this game most likely. They went through my pockets pulling out my wallet, my keys, and my passport. The laid each item on the hood of their truck as they continued to pad me down. They had me remove my jacket and put that on the truck also.

"Do you have any drugs on you?" they asked me.

"No señor, I am forty-five years old and do not take any drugs," I responded.

The driver seemed to have the bulk of the attitude and forensically took apart my wallet.

"Where are you staying?" the passenger cop asked me. "What are you doing here?" He seemed both accusing and interested at the same time.

"I'm staying at the Cascadas hotel." I pointed to the hotel placard and my room key. "I'm here on vacation, enjoying some beers and some ladies. Is that OK? Do you not like American tourists?" I asked him.

"No we like them," he said. "But many Americans come down to purchase drugs."

"I'm sure," I said as the other gentleman finished going though all my things.

"You two should join me at Adelita's after work tonight," I invited. "I'll buy you a drink."

The nicer of the cops said he just might, and the other cop just handed me my stuff and glared at me as I walked away. He was mad their little trap had failed, and I was laughing inside at their stupid attempt. The mouse was smarter than the cat in this instance. I had hidden the cheese, I thought. Still, that was close. No more buying drugs in Mexico. The cops and the drug dealers are often working together...just like in LA, I thought. The difference is I could have bought these cops off for a couple hundred bucks, and the American police would have stolen everything I had and destroyed my life. Yup, Mexican cops are better, I thought. Jeez, the sad world of reality…

Well, after all that excitement, I was ready for a beer and perhaps some company to burn off my anxiety.

I thought about Hong Kong and Barbie, which didn't sound bad, but I was here for adventure, not a relationship, so I opted for Adelita's.

When I entered, the place was packed wall to wall. There were at least a hundred women standing along the walkways and circled around the stage. As I rounded a corner, a tiny, little, petite girl caught my eye. She was standing in a group of other ladies and was quite a bit smaller than them. She wore a yellow outfit and seemed to be quite shy. I always liked the shy ones. They tend to be very teachable in bed.

Still, I didn't want to make eye contact until I had thoroughly checked her out, so I walked around behind to get a different perspective. OK, it was official. She was cute as a button. I walked up behind her and asked her if she would like a drink. She accepted.

Now the waiters in these places always keep an eye on the girls and when they are approached by a guy, the waiter always pounces into action.

I ordered her a drink, and the waiter found us a spot near the bar. Only one stool, but he sat me down than nudged the girl to sit on my lap. A photographer offered to take our picture, which I allowed and then paid him ten dollars for the instamatic photo. She was so tiny I barely felt her, but what I did feel felt good. She looked at me with big, sleepy, sexy eyes and gave me a kiss on the neck. As we talked, I found out her name was Angela, and she was twenty-two years old. She also told me this was her very first night and that she was from Tabasco, Mexico. Now I had heard of tabasco sauce, but I didn't know it actually came from Mexico.

We had our drinks, and both decided it was time to go upstairs. I took her by the hand, and we walked to the door.

This girl was very sweet and very shy but also very affectionate. We kissed in the elevator and down the hall to my room. Inside, we laid on the bed together as I slowly removed her shoes and her clothing. I felt so connected as I kissed her whole body, one kiss at a time. I decided to enter her without a condom. She felt wet and very tight. She asked me to please go slow, which I gladly did. I wanted this to be romantic, not just fucking. I could tell at one point she began to come, and her body convulsed. I continued a long, slow, stroking motion and rolled her over. I've always been more of a butt guy anyway. I started increasing in rhythm and asked her if I could go faster now as I felt my body become inflamed with ecstasy.

She said, "Yes," so I unleashed on her. She grabbed the sheets with both hands as I thrusted her toward the headboard. Sweat started dripping on her back from my overheated body. I asked her if she was ready and then finished inside her.

Immediately after, I fell to the bed exhausted. I asked her if she could spend the night with me, and she said I would have to pay the bar the $300 exit fee but that she wouldn't charge me anything. I agreed. Throughout the night, we continued our romantic encounter. I really liked this girl.

In the morning, I had to leave by 9:00 a.m., so I woke up Angela and told her we had to go. We got in the shower together, which gave me the perfect opportunity to enjoy her again. She was so sensual and very compliant. As I took her downstairs, we decided to share a cab. She said she lived nearby in an area called "Colonia Independencia."

As we drove in the car, I didn't want to leave her. When the cab parked in front of her house, she kissed me one more time and then shocked the hell out of me.

"Dalton, listen to me. I love you, Dalton. Whenever you visit me, I am no longer working, OK? I only work to pay for my brother's school. When he becomes a doctor, he will pay for my school. If you ever want me to stop working, I just need to pay for his school and have a place to live. His school is only $200 per month. I love you, Dalton."

With that, she kissed me and got out of the cab. I gave her a hundred dollars "for her expenses" as she would not accept it for her services. She was for real.

My head was spinning. What the hell was going on? I had just come down for a good time, not to fall in love. Now two girls were claiming me?

"Wow, I love this country," I thought as I made my way back to the border.

The line was over an hour long to get back across. Four hours later, I was back to the dispensary. It was Monday, I was feeling refreshed, and Lorraine was visiting tonight. Wow, I hadn't had this much action since my twenties, I thought.

"Back to the real world," I thought as I entered the dispensary. When I entered, it was about noon, and Skip was sitting playing chess with Joshua, who was supposed to be the bud tender today. I walked back into the dispensary and noticed a lot of the prep work was not done, and my "Wheel of Fortune" had been removed. I called Skip to the back and asked him what was going on. He told me he and Josh had decided to stop doing the wheel because we were giving away too many joints, and it was a lot of work rolling them.

"So we've got time to play chess, but we don't have time to roll joints for the customers?" I asked.

"Well, we can still do it on the weekends," Skip suggested. I bit my lip and walked upstairs. I was paying Skip and Josh a lot of money to sit and play chess. When I came down later to review sales, I noticed a distinct decline.

When I asked Skip and Josh about this, Josh kind of got an attitude and told me our prices were too high, and people didn't want to come to a "Chuck E. Cheese" dispensary. I started to understand the problem was that we had a lazy bud tender and manager. Our customer service was failing, and this person didn't believe in our concept. When the five o'clock shift came in, I called Skip and Josh into the office.

"Josh, you are being relieved of your duties," I told him. "Skip, I am writing you up with a warning. I decide the policies in my store, and if you don't want to work in a Chuck E. Cheese, then there is the door. Skip, take the rest of the night off and Josh, hit the door."

Needless to say, Josh was pissed. He shouted insults on his way out the door to the point that I told him if he didn't leave, I'd have the cops escort him out. He finally left.

Skip said nothing other than, "I'm going out." He stayed out the whole night.

Chapter 13: Council Bluffs
November 2009

The city council had put together a hasty new ordinance and was going to shove it down our throats. They scheduled a sham public hearing, to which again four hundred advocates showed up. They again limited us to fifteen seconds, which is about the time it takes for you to announce yourself and say "hello."

I called another meeting of GAPP, and this time over a hundred members showed. I had become somewhat of a celebrity in the industry. Everyone was gaining courage, and we were going on the offence for the first time. We decided to attack the new ordinance itself.

Now I must admit I was very naive when it came to petitions, especially in LA. Everything in LA feels like it is rigged in the government's favor. Once I filed the required documents, the city attorney had up to ten days to review it. After that, we had twenty more days to gather all the signatures. What a crock of shit. At the next GAPP meeting, we instructed all the dispensaries to start gathering the signatures of registered voters only.

Of course, the city took the entire ten days to review our petition, only to send it back to us with some minor errors. By the time we finally had gotten it approved, we had less than twenty days. Despite our best efforts, we were only able to collect 15,000 signatures instead of the required 24,000.. We asked for an extension but were denied. Typical City Hall.

I did, however, attract the attention of a PAC who began educating me on how things really worked in LA. To successfully do a petition, you basically had to buy the signatures. Depending on how much you were willing to pay and how much political action was occurring, you could get it done for anywhere from $1 to $2 per verified signature. In other words, if we were willing to pay $24,000 to $48,000, we would be assured the petition would make it. Isn't America great?

* * *

I got a call from an old friend, and he said he wanted to come visit me in LA. This guy was as straight laced as they come, and he had worked for me for many years as the manager of my Adventure Club for singles back in Phoenix. I asked him if he was sure he actually wanted to visit and stay in a pot shop and he said sure, as long as I didn't try to hire him.

I promised I wouldn't. Now Fred was a big gentle guy who didn't believe in drugs and didn't like stoners. I always said he had Fred Flintstone looks with a Barney Rubble personality.

He came over the Thanksgiving holidays, and I treated the entire staff to a nice dinner at a restaurant. I was surprised Lorraine agreed to come as my date. She had started hinting around lately that she might be looking for a relationship, and I wasn't quite sure how I felt about that. My mind was always on Angela since the day I had met her in Mexico, but I was enjoying being single and a player at forty-five. "Why change?" I thought.

Fred only came out for three days, but after meeting my staff and interacting with my customers, he left with a smile and a wink.

"If you ever need someone, let me know. I think I could work here," he said.

I said I'd keep that in mind. Fred was honest, hardworking, and didn't smoke weed. He might be the perfect manager, I thought. Skip was becoming more and more undependable and business kept slipping. I had started getting complaints from customers, but my staff loved him so I kept him onboard. I invited him to stay through the Christmas holidays. He accepted.

It would be hard firing an old high school buddy.

Chapter 14: Feliz Navidad
2009

With Christmas soon approaching, I decided to throw a Christmas party for the employees before heading down to Mexico to see Angela before she returned to see her family in Tabasco. We decided to have the event at our favorite watering hole, The Good Hurt, and everyone was allowed to bring their significant other.

I had a dilemma. Should I invite Lorraine as my "sure thing" or take a chance and see if anything panned out with Susan that night? Tits McGee was another possibility as she had been making some hints lately that maybe we should be dating. Too many women, so little time. Brittany was coming also with her ass crack on full display, I'm sure, but recently she and Fred had been hanging out. Fred was thirty years her senior, and I had been coaching him to just get high with her and let things happen.

Fred had never gotten high in his life, so this definitely took some coaching.

I decided to go with the safe choice and invited Lorraine. Also, I knew that a good strategy for getting a woman to pursue you was to show up with another attractive woman and make them compete. This plan never fails and was on full display that night.

Sure enough, when Susan arrived, she saw I was sitting with Lorraine and came over to introduce herself. Luckily, there were no other chairs close by, so I looked over at Fred and motioned for him to get her a chair on the other side of the table from me. I had briefed Fred on the plan hours earlier, so he definitely knew what was up. Susan had no problem mingling, obviously, but I could tell she really wanted to make her way back to this end of the table. I pretended not to notice. I could tell Tits McGee also noticed the competition, and I caught a couple mean glares coming our way. My plan was working perfectly. I paid full attention to Lorraine, which was never hard to do.

Britany, Karen, Sagi, and Eric all filtered in through the door. Marco showed up a half hour late, as usual. Passion had recently accepted a modeling job in France and so would not be joining us. We all proceeded to drink and dance our way into oblivion. I didn't really notice when Susan left, but sometime after 2:00 a.m., Lorraine and I stumbled down the street and made our way to the apartment. I could hear Fred and Brittany going at it upstairs, so everyone was definitely having a Merry Christmas.

The next day, Lorraine awoke early and snuck out as usual. She was really embarrassed to think anyone knew she had stayed and didn't like walking out past the employees when they were working. The walk of shame, as she called it. Fred and Brittany were still in their room, so I knocked and told Fred I would be headed to Mexico. A muffled "OK" came out of the room.

With that, I jumped on the 405 and headed south. Now, it was Sunday morning, and I had planned to spend a couple days with Angela. The thing about Angela, for me, was that I not only felt like her boyfriend but also like a father figure to her. You see, both of her parents had died when she was very young, and you could just tell she had never really had anyone to dote over her. The person she called her brother was actually her cousin, and the person she called mother was her aunt. When they both spoke on the phone, it was almost always a tear fest.

For her twenty-second birthday, I threw her a surprise party and bought a large Winnie the Pooh and Eeyore stuffed animals, as well as all the party decorations. I had her wait in the bedroom, while I decorated and lit the cake. Once it was ready, I brought her out and yelled, "Surprise!" Her eyes welled up with tears as she sat down in disbelief. I wanted to give her more days like that.

So I had some big plans for her, including buying her a promise ring with a small diamond. I wanted her to know how special she was. Traffic heading south was lighter than normal, so I made good time. I was at Angela's house within about three hours of leaving. As soon as she opened the door, I picked her up and carried her to the couch and removed her clothing. I guess the anticipation of the drive had gotten the better of me, and I had to have her then and now. Afterward, we decided to go out for lunch and found a great grilled chicken place in one of the neighborhoods. That's the amazing thing about Mexico; you can find great food on almost every street corner.

A few weeks prior, I had bought a small Christmas tree for her apartment and was slowly amassing gifts. As night fell on Christmas Eve, I set up my video camera and put on some Christmas music. Now in my family, it was tradition to open gifts on Christmas Day, but most Mexican families did it on Christmas Eve. When in Rome, do as the Romans do, right?

With the video rolling, one by one Angela opened her gifts. You could tell she was very shy and uncomfortable to be receiving so many. She gave me a shirt that she really liked, and she had me try it on.

Once all the gifts were open, I had Angela stand up and I began to remove her clothing. My gift to myself was that I wanted to have a video of her naked body all over me, in front of the tree. At first, she was compliant, but then she suddenly remembered the video was running and started squirming to cover up. It was too late; I had her where I wanted her. She struggled for a few more seconds, then gave into the passion of the moment. I got thirty minutes of great video, enjoying Angela from all angles.

When we were exhausted, she again remembered the video and made me promise, "No internet."

Nope, this was for me and me alone.

Now the strip clubs in Tijuana go twenty-four seven, three hundred sixty-five days per year, so they are even open on Christmas day. When Angela and I were bored, we would sometimes go down and check out the other clubs, so we decided to go for a few hours. Angela had some girlfriends who worked at another club called Chicago Club, so we went down to that one for a while. Whenever we saw her girlfriends, Angela would make sure I bought them drinks so they could get tickets, which I did happily.

After leaving Chicago Club, we decided to walk down to a club called Purple Rain, which sometimes had some decent girls and acts. We walked in and got a table right next to the stage. I ordered two beers and a shot for me. Angela had one of those personalities that change dramatically after a couple beers, so I had to pace her slowly. The first girl was rather large and unattractive, so I spent most of my time doting on Angela and kissing her. Our second round of beers came and, all of a sudden, I saw Angela's eyes perk up. I looked in the direction she was looking, expecting to see a guy or something but no…She was all perked up looking at a young healthy female Daltoncer with crazy curly hair walking out on the stage. The girl strutted right in front of us and captivated the whole room in an instant. She wrapped her leg around the pole and began to spin her body until she was laying down on the floor right in front of us. Her sexy legs sprawled in our direction, with her eyes looking directly at us. Now I was trying to play it cool and not give the girl too much attention because there is nothing worse than a drunken, jealous, Hispanic woman, but when I looked at Angela to see if I had been busted, I swear she was more enthralled with this young lady than I was. I offered Angela a dollar to give this girl a tip, and Angela happily stood up and slid the dollar into the girl's G-string. From Angela's mannerisms, I could tell she was very attracted to the girl, which threw me for a loop. I had no idea Angela might like women also.

"Hmmm, this could get interesting," I thought.

"Te gusta?" I inquired, asking her if she liked this girl.

"Ella es muy hermosa," she replied, confirming my eager suspicions. I could tell she was shy about admitting this and a little embarrassed, but I kept pushing.

"You like girls?" I asked, in Spanish, of course.

"I've never tried," she told me. "But I think so."

Then she just blew my mind with her next statement. She basically told me that she knows I am a man and that men like multiple women. She told me that she was going to be leaving for a month, and she didn't want me to be alone while she was gone. She told me that if I wanted to invite this girl back to her apartment tonight, that she was fine with that.

I was at a loss for words. "Is this a test?" I wondered. "Or did I just fall in love with the most amazing woman to ever walk the planet?"

I needed to proceed with caution. I had to put the decision back on her. I didn't want to seem too anxious.

"Baby, I think it's obvious you like this girl. I agree she is very sexy. If you want to invite her back to the apartment, I will support your decision. I just want you to be happy always, my love. Do you want to invite her, mi carino? Why don't we invite her to our table and see where this goes?" I suggested. My life had just gotten a thousand times more interesting.

Angela stood up and whispered in the dancer's ear, and she looked at me and nodded. She sat down on the edge of the stage and straddled me, so I lifted her up and sat her on my lap. She gave me a big kiss, then bent over and kissed Angela. I ordered shots for the table and began enjoying the company of both ladies.

We found out her name was Victoria, and she was from Chihuahua, Mexico. She had only been working and living in Tijuana for two weeks and was twenty-three years old. Her shift ended at midnight, and then we all grabbed a cab back to Angela's house. Angela was more than a little tipsy at this point, and I basically had to carry her out of the bar. I could see the respect in the waiter's eyes that I was leaving with two gorgeous women. Machismo is a big deal in Mexico. A man who can handle two women is "el toro"—the bull.

Outside the bar, a taxi was waiting and I held the door for Victoria, then placed Angela after me. I gave the instructions to the driver and then began to explore my newfound treat. Angela was two sheets to the wind and basically fell asleep as I explored every inch of Victoria's young, hard body.

The taxi stopped in front of Angela's house and we were greeted by Manches, the landlord's poodle. He had become familiar with me so only barked once then came to be petted. By this point, Angela was stone cold, so I put her over my shoulder and carried her with Victoria by my side. I searched through Angela's purse, when we got to the door and found the keys on top. I had Victoria open the door and carried Angela to the bedroom. I laid her down like a sack of potatoes. Victoria and I smiled at each other as we closed the door to Angela's room.

I pushed Victoria against the wall, and we made out passionately for a few minutes. I tried to lead her to the couch, but she motioned that she needed to take a shower first. Understandable, as she had been Dancing all night and I'm sure felt very dirty. I loved how clean the girls always kept themselves down here.

I found a fresh towel for her and then watched as she removed her clothing and stepped into the shower. By then, I was so worked up that I thought "Why wait?" and I disrobed and stepped into the shower also.

Victoria was pleasantly surprised, and we spent the next thirty minutes slipping and sliding around the bathtub. This girl was amazing.

Finally, when we had our fill, we both exited and dried off. I took the towel and sponged off every inch of her body, with many stops along the way. Her skin was much darker than Angela's, her hair was full of dark, tight curls, and her lips were full and inviting. Her nipples were the color of dark chocolate and responded quickly to kissing and touch. Once dry, we both went into Angela's bedroom. Angela didn't move. We each laid on one side of Angela, and our hands met over her warm body. Best Christmas ever, I thought, but the best was yet to come.

I'm an early riser, so at about 6:00 a.m., as the sun poked through the window, I saw my beautiful bounty from the night before. In a few short minutes, my whole body was alive and on the prowl. Now Angela was always a heavy sleeper and definitely not a morning person, but she never turned down a good morning fuck, which is what I was about to give her. I looked over at Victoria and her back was to me but exposed. I could see her perfect little backside all the way down to her ass. I decided to get Angela excited first and then get Victoria to join in once initiated. Slowly, I started kissing Angela's neck and back. She moved slowly at first but then remembered the familiar morning drill.

She was a woman who believed it was her duty to satisfy her man, and she never let me down. Now Angela was so tiny, you really had to get her wet before you could enter her. Luckily I found some lube on the side of the bed. I loved waking her up with me inside her, watching her eyes come to life and her nipples become hard as she realized what was occurring.

Once she was sufficiently awake, I motioned over to Victoria and took Angela's hand over to touch her. She started rubbing Victoria's back very delicately. Victoria began to stir a bit. At that point, I decided it was time to wake up Victoria, so I slid out of Angela and made my way over to her sleeping body. Angela started kissing her back as I took a generous helping of lubricant and warmed it up on my fingers.

Once warmed, I placed the lube on my man part and then slid myself into Victoria from behind. Her body shuddered with surprise and pleasure. Within a few minutes, she rolled onto her back, so I could get deeper inside her. She and Angela began kissing as I took turns switching back and forth. I honestly think Angela was enjoying this more than I was and at one point, she went down on Victoria as I nailed her from behind. Victoria kept repeating, "This is just like a porno movie."

She was right. This was beyond my wildest dreams, and everything seemed to move in slow motion. We spent the better part of the day taking turns, eating, drinking, and sleeping. Day turned to night, and Victoria said she had to go to work, so we had one more go-around and then she left. Angela and I collapsed, exhausted as hell.

The next morning, I drove back to Los Angeles. Back to the battle with the dishonest politicians and the sleepless nights. A big part of me wanted to just buy a condo in Mexico and live in this fantasy world, free of the pressures of the American way of life. The fighter in me forced me to return and to get ready for the battle ahead.

"Feliz Navidad," I thought.

Chapter 15: Petition Fails
January to February 2010

Our petition failed, and the new ordinance came into effect. John Hoffman of the *LA Times* walked with me to the recorder's office and took photos as I turned in the petitions. He wrote another article about me failing at the petition, making us look like a bunch of disorganized, scrappy organizers.

March 2010

Our sales were tanking and, as best as I could tell, Skip was doing nothing to change that. His attitude sucked, and he was only here for a pay check. I called Fred and offered him the position, and he jumped at the change. He was still living in Arizona but said he could be there in three days.

With that, I planned to not fire Skip but to get him out of the dispensary and start looking for grow locations. To break the news to him, I decided to take him on a Mexico trip with me, all expenses paid. After all, he was an old buddy and we had some catching up to do.

We made the drive to Mexico and got checked into our hotel at about 5:00 p.m. We went down to the bar and very quickly a girl approached Skip. She was a somewhat chunky, not so attractive female that looked like she had busted out a few kids. I tried to get Skip to hold off as there were more girls coming later, but he was excited about this one, so they started having drinks. After two drinks and two shots, they decide to go up to Skip's room. I told him I would be sitting right here when he returned.

Half an hour went by, then an hour. Finally, I saw the girl appear in the doorway but no Skip. When I asked her where he was, she told me he was sleeping. I went up to his room, and he answered all drunk and sleepy.

"Yeah, I'm crashing," he said and he closed the door.

That was the last I saw of him until morning. Jeez, what a lightweight, I thought.

It was only 6:00 p.m., and Angela wasn't supposed to show until 9:00 p.m., so I had some time to kill. I decided to walk around the block. On the back side of the strip clubs, there was an alleyway with literally hundreds of girls of all shapes and sizes. The prices were much cheaper in the alley, and for twenty dollars, you could get a real hottie. I decided what the heck and picked out a tall, dark skin girl with blond highlights. You could tell by her body she was quite the athlete. Best twenty bucks I ever spent.

Later, Angela showed up and we spent the rest of the night together in the bar or in my room. I received the complete girlfriend treatment whenever we were together. When she got off work at 3:00 a.m., she invited me to come spend that night at her house, so that's where we went. I was absolutely shocked to see what she had on the mantle of the fireplace. It was the photo of the first time we had met. Wow, I guess when she said she loved me, she meant it. I was starting to feel that way also. She was different. Special.

At about 9:00 a.m., I got a text from Skip, so I gave Angela a morning pounding, then jumped in a cab. God, I loved banging her in the morning before she was barely awake. Her arms and legs would get goosebumps as her nipples grew hard as a rock.

I got back to the hotel, and Skip was still gimping around.

"You look like you need a beer," I said.

"Yeah right," he said. "No thanks."

"Damn lightweight. You telling me you are one and done?" I asked. "You don't have any morning wood?"

"Nah, my stomach is sour," he said.

"Let's go to the pharmacy," I suggested.

Checkout was 11:00 a.m., so we packed up our suitcases and left them with the concierge.

"Are they safe?" Skip asked.

"Absolutely," I told him.

After picking him up some Pepto-Bismol tablets, we returned to the bar.

"We still have some time to kill," I told him as I ordered a beer.

We sat near the dance stage, and a beautiful young dancer came out to entertain us. The music started blaring. This girl had long, natural blond hair. Definitely from Guadalajara. Her perfectly fit body had a generous helping of cleavage but not too much. Her dance was very seductive, and she ended up crouching on the ground like a tiger during a Shakira song and prowling toward our table on all fours. She was definitely on the hunt, and my "hot pussy" meter started to go off.

"Oh god, Skip, somebody needs to fuck this poor girl," I said. "She is working way too hard for this and looks way too good."

"Go for it," he said, his belly still aching from his two drinks the night before.

"Well, a man's got to do what a man's got to do," I said. I pointed upstairs, and the girl met me at the door.

She was not kidding. She was indeed a tiger.

I finished up my work in the bedroom and jumped down to get Skip. This last minute diversion had put us behind. I wanted to cross the border before I gave Skip the bad news. Our bonding evening didn't go quite as planned. Even Brian had been more fun.

Once we crossed the border, we decided to eat at a Denny's, which I thought would be the perfect environment. I had scoped out a few possible grow locations online, and Skip and I were supposed to check them out that day. I got a text message that Fred had arrived at the Rainforest, so I knew the store was secure.

As we sat down, I ordered the steak and eggs. All that sex had made me hungry. Skip just got a water.

I decided it was time to break the news to him.

"All right, Skip, well just to let you know, I wanted to hang out together last night because I have something to tell you."

"OK," he said with confusion in his eyes.

"I've hired a new manager for the Rainforest, Fred Fink. You might remember he visited during Thanksgiving?"

"He doesn't know anything about pot," he said, with disgust and contempt. "How's that gonna work?"

"He doesn't need to know anything about pot. He knows about customer service. The customers already know what they like. We do not need to educate them. There's plenty of information online," I stated.

"So I'm just done?" He said.

"Well, no," I said. "I brought you here from Michigan to run a grow for me, not to run the dispensary in the first place. That's why we are here. I have a couple locations lined up today."

"You know what, I'm just gonna hop a train, go pick up my stuff at the shop, and bug out," he said.

"That's an option also," I said. "I'm not gonna have my business run into the ground."

"Fine," he said. "Then that's what we will do. Tell Fred I'm on my way, that damn snake."

"I will," I said.

Skip stomped out. I immediately called Fred and informed him to walk Skip to the door and get all of his keys. Actually, we should call a locksmith just in case. We got the whole place rekeyed and the alarm codes changed.

Chapter 16: A New Direction

Fred was trained quickly. At first, the staff was upset that Skip was gone and gave Fred the cold shoulder. They agreed he had no experience, and they all objected to the way Skip was terminated.

But Fred was my secret weapon. He was a friendly, helpful guy who always had a stupid joke to tell. He and I had run an adult activity club together, so we had all kinds of ideas for events and gatherings for the employees and patients. We started having game night and grow classes.

Before Skip, our sales were around $10,000 per week. By the time Skip and Josh had run our business into the ground, we were at $2,500 per week and barely breaking even.

Quickly, attitudes changed, and all the staff and patients fell in love with Fred. Our sales recovered back to their pre-Skip levels.

One night, Lorraine came to see me, and it seemed that some anonymous caller had contacted her and told her I was hanging out with "whores" in Mexico. She wasn't so upset about this as she was that someone had gotten her personal information. I called a meeting with the staff and rebuked them as a group. "How dare they release this info?" I said.

But it was obviously Skip trying to get revenge. He had always had an attraction for Lorraine. He didn't understand that Lorraine and I were nonexclusive by agreement. That didn't mean she was interested in him. He was kind of a jerk, to be honest.

I received another letter from Stephen Cooley's district attorney office. This letter gave everyone a deadline to close by June 9, or they would be raided and arrested. That gave us two months to do something, so I called David Welch for a meeting.

Of all the attorneys I had spoken to, he was the least well known but seemed to me to be the smartest by far. He could always recite the laws that the city was violating and seemed to know what we should do about it.

"What should we do, David? Tell me," I said.

"Well, Dalton, I've been telling you. We need to file a lawsuit. The city is trying to use zoning to shut you down, but they can't do that without proper zoning maps in place, and they know it."

"I know, David, but lawsuits are expensive, and nobody has millions of dollars to spend. The city has unlimited resources. Let me ask you, David. If I were able to put together eighty dispensaries how much would you charge me, per dispensary, flat rate, from beginning to end, to prosecute our case against the city? And keep this in mind, David, I will make you famous by getting your name in the *Wall Street Journal*, the *LA Times*, *The Associated Press*, and more. Every time they call me, I will reference you as my attorney."

David smiled. He knew the type of publicity would skyrocket his visibility in a city already drowning in tens of thousands of attorneys. He was quick to come back with his answer.

"I will charge you $5000 each, beginning to end, plus court costs."

"If I can put that together, can we win this, David?"

"I think so. I will have to add staff, but yes, we can win this," he assured me.

"Then let's do this."

I shook his hand, and the deal was done.

We called another meeting of the GAPP. I stated our case, Mark gave his opinion, and David Welch knocked it out of the park. The group went crazy. He collected forty new clients that night alone and continued to add clients for weeks moving forward. We were suing the city of Los Angeles.

Other attorneys across the city brought their clients and joined us in the suit. When we had our lawsuit prepared, I called the *LA Times* and the *Wall Street Journal*. We rocked the news with our new offensive.

April 2010

I was now seeing Angela on a regular basis, almost every weekend. This weekend, we had gotten a room done in Rosita Beach and rented some horses to ride up and down the beach. She had shown up in her typical high heels, so I took her to buy some sandals at one of the beach shops.

We had dinner at a beach bar called Papas and Beer, which is a popular tourist spot on the beach. As it started to get busy, we decided to go back to the room and just be alone. That was never boring.

Angela had had a lot to drink by the time we got to the room and had gotten surprisingly feisty and frisky. We walked out onto the seventh floor balcony, and Angela decided she wanted to have sex right then and there on the balcony...so I obliged her. We went to bed early and slept well. I always slept so well in Mexico, with Angela by my side.

In the morning, we decided to take a walk down the beach at around 10:00 a.m. There, many beach vendors were selling their wares, and I bought Angela a small bracelet.

About 10:30 a.m., my phone rang. It was Fred on the line.

"OK, Dalton. I have something to tell you, but I don't want you to worry because nobody's hurt," he said.

"OK," I said, quite alarmed.

"We were just robbed at gunpoint," he informed me. "They came in the front door right at 10:00 a.m. as we opened. April was working out front. There were two of them. The one who had the gun stayed out front. They took April's key and locked her in the smoking lounge so she went and hid in the apartment and locked both doors. Brittany was in the bud room as the younger guy came in and announced that Dalton had to told him to clean the buds. He proceeded to grab jars of bud from the shelves and put them in a duffle bag. As soon as he walked into the man cage, he was trapped. Brittany ran back to the office where I was counting money. I grabbed the taser gun and reentered the bud room. I could see on the video screens that the man out front was trying desperately to break his friend out of the cage. I could not see April, so I assumed they had taken her hostage. I pushed the silent alarm and announced I had a gun back here. They said they had a gun, too. Somehow, they managed to break him out of the man cage before the cops arrived. The cops are here now. I gave them a copy of the surveillance tape. I think they shot the lock off, but the police say they didn't."

I was stunned. Well, that was the end of that trip. I took Angela home and headed to LA.

We were up and running the next day. April was a little shaken but OK. The cops never followed up with us on this. The LAPD was too busy committing crimes to go after criminals. They would rather bust someone with marijuana than go after a bad guy with a gun.

These type of robberies were becoming more common. Just the week prior, another store was robbed that had an armed security guard. The guard had his arm broken but had managed to get a bullet into one of the robbers. I guess the trail of blood stained the sidewalk for blocks.

"Good," I thought. "I hope he dies."

Many of us believed we were being attacked by a joint task force of the LAPD, federal agents, and cartels.

A few nights later, I was pulling into the back parking spaces when I was approached by two small Hispanic guys. Luckily, I had just gotten the gates locked by the time they reached me.

"Hey, homie," they said. "We've got some weed we want to sell in your store, man. Can we come in and talk to you?"

I could tell these guys were gang members and were looking to scare me.

"I hear you are making some powerful enemies, bro. We would hate for anything to happen to you or your little employees," they said.

"Jose Huizar says hi," they said as they left. "Don't make us come back."

Huizar was known for keeping lists of his enemies and intimidating them. Ten years later, he would be arrested for racketeering and selling favors. Who knew? I did. I can tell a snake when I see one.

"OK, now things are getting dangerous," I thought, but I wasn't scared. "This is living…"

Sex, drugs, and crooked cops. It was like reading a spy book, except I was the main character.

My girlfriend had once said she thought I had a "death wish." I can think back many times in my life where she was right. Ukraine had been dangerous, Tijuana was dangerous, and LA was dangerous, but I felt alive.

Later that evening, Susan stopped by around 6:00 p.m. and asked if we could talk about something. She told me she hadn't had any work in a while and was representing a few strains. I told her I would look at them, but to be honest, I already had way too much weed and the price of weed had been dropping dramatically. We went back into the smoking lounge and she pulled out some different types of bud, about midlevel quality. Her price was way too high, and I told her I wouldn't be able to buy any that night. I could see the disappointment, but she understood. We smoked a bowl together as I told her about the day's events with the narcos threatening me and all the stress of the week. I told her I hadn't been sleeping well and kept having nightmares about raids and really weird stuff.

"You know," Susan said, as she got up off the couch and sat directly behind me to my left. "I've been known to give very good massages, and I am a great stress reliever also."

Her strong hands clamped onto my shoulders, delivering extreme pressure to my sore, aching muscles.

"Maybe we can help each other out," she proposed.

"What did you have in mind?" I asked, already knowing the answer. My body became alive and full of testosterone as I had been fantasizing about her since the first time we met.

"Well I say, why don't we go upstairs and let me relieve all of your stress and you can just buy my weed on consignment. Pay me when you sell it," she offered. "I promise I'm very good at what I do."

"How can I say no to that offer?" I agreed as I stood up and started leading her to my apartment. She spent the next two hours fulfilling my Susan, porn star fantasy. I was not disappointed. By about 9:00 p.m., we both had had our fill, and I personally had a ravenous hunger.

"You up for sushi?" I asked. "You've been working hard, young lady."

"Let's do it, I'm starving," Susan said enthusiastically.

With that, we stumbled around looking for miscellaneous articles of clothing. We never did find her panties.

We headed down the block on foot to a nearby sushi place. When we arrived, we were surprised to see that it was almost completely full. I went to the hostess stand, and they informed me it would be a forty-minute wait. I surveyed the room and saw a cramped little table with two seats and lo and behold, who was sitting there but Bill Rosendahl, our city councilman.

I thought this might be the opportunity I was looking for, so I told the hostess I was meeting Bill and that she could sit me right next to him if she liked. Being young, she took the bait and guided me right through to his table. I took Susan by the hand, and we worked our way through the crowded dining room.

As we arrived, I acknowledged Bill and reminded him I was the dispensary owner in his district. Once he recollected, he motioned for me to sit down at the two empty spots and we were in. Mission accomplished. Sometimes, you have to think fast.

Susan leaned over, her braless chest semi-exposed, and said, "Damn, that was impressive."

"I just got lucky," I said.

The waitress arrived quickly, and we ordered some hot sake and Sapporo beers. As we waited, I took my first glance at Bill's dinner partner. Now remember, Bill was in his sixties, with a large frame and poor eyesight. The young man across from him had to be in his young twenties and was Hispanic. You could tell by his feminine mannerisms and clothing choices that he was Bill's boy-toy. They were holding hands across the table, and Bill kept whispering to him.

The bar was loud and noisy, so it was hard to strike up a conversation, but I reminded Bill again who I was and handed him my card.

"Bill, if you need anything, just call me and I will deliver."

"Well, I appreciate that, Dalton," he said. "Will you be around later tonight?"

"Absolutely, Bill. I'll be up until about 2:00 a.m."

"Good to know," Bill said. He and his date left shortly thereafter, and Susan and I wolfed down many plates of uncooked fishes of all types. I guess we had both worked up quite an appetite. I looked at Susan; her sweat-drenched hair hung down limp to the side of her head.

"God, she's so hot" I thought. Then I realized we had never even kissed the whole time we engaged. "Porn stars must not like kissing," I thought.

We finished our meal, and both walked back to the dispensary. Susan said she had to get going, and I gave her a consignment form for her weed that she had left. Once I walked her out to the car, my phone began vibrating, so I gave Susan a hug as she got in the car and drove away.

It was close to midnight and I normally wouldn't answer an unknown caller, but I kind of thought I might know who it was.

"Hey Dalton, it's Bill Rosendahl. I'm calling to take you up on your offer," he confided.

"Great, Bill. What can I get you? It's on me."

"Well, my friend Mario would like some smoke, but I'm more into the edibles, so whatever you think is appropriate," Bill said.

"OK, Bill, I will hook you right up with a care package and be over in about fifteen to twenty minutes. How does that sound?" I asked.

"Sounds fantastic," Bill said. "See you soon."

"OK, great. Just please be near the door because the battery on my phone is dying, and I may not be able to call you."

"I will, Dalton. Thanks."

With that, I walked back into the dispensary, grabbed a bag, and stated packing it with goodies. I really wanted to impress Bill with our selection and quality. I gave him a couple brownies, a couple cookies, and my favorite gummy bears. For Mario, I threw in a top-of-the-line sativa and a purple indica. I also included a small pipe and a free lighter. It was not every day that you got to do an illegal drug deal with a city council member, I thought.

Bill's house was in walking distance, so I made my way out the back door, through the gate, and down the alley. When I arrived, there was one light on downstairs and one light upstairs. I rang the bell, and Bill popped the door open immediately.

"Brownie delivery service," I said.

"Oh, Dalton. Thank you, thank you. You just made my night. How much do I owe you?"

"It's a gift, Bill," I said as I raised my hand, waving off his cash.

"Well, thank you Dalton," he said again.

With that, he closed the door, and I headed back to the dispensary. As I was making my way to the back alley, I noticed a low rider car sitting on the other side of the alleyway. It was running and seemed to have two occupants. They definitely didn't look like they belonged in the area. Now I do not get spooked often, but I thought it better that I walk out to Venice Boulevard where there was lots of traffic. I decided to duck into my neighbor's liquor store and perhaps pick up some smokes and see if my good friend Emmanuel was working. We spoke for a few minutes, and then I walked back out onto the street. There it was. The same car was now parked on the boulevard about three car lengths from the front door of the Rainforest.

"Probably nothing," I thought. As I got to the door, I kept one eye on them as I fumbled for the keys. They remained in the car. I popped the key in, and the door opened immediately. I was quite happy to close the door behind me and pull the bars closed. "I'm just being paranoid," I told myself.

As I walked through the dark front lobby, I noticed that someone had propped the man cage open from the front, which the employees sometimes did. I was going back to the bud room anyway, so I removed the chair as I entered the cage. The door closed quickly behind me. Then it hit me.

Did I just lock myself in the man cage? I ran to the opposite door and sure enough, it was locked. I couldn't believe I just did that. Here I was at 1:00 a.m. and the only person in the store. I was locked in a cage, and nobody would be there until about 9:30 a.m. tomorrow. I grabbed for my phone real quick and, of course, my battery had just died.

"Oh well, I guess I'm sleeping on this cold hard floor tonight," I thought. All I had were the clothes on my back to comfort me. I took off my shirt and my pants, so I could make some type of bedding. I laid down on the hard makeshift bed, just thinking about how the employees would come in the next day to discover their half-naked boss lying on the floor.

"How could things get any worse?" I thought. "And after such a great day." Then I felt the gurgle. Then I felt another gurgle coming from my abdomen.

"Oh no, are you kidding me?" Mother nature was calling at the exact wrong time. I had no choice but to answer, and now I had to use my clothing to clean up and cover the mess. It almost seems funny now. Me locked in a cage, half naked, with human feces and all the smells that go with that. Needless to say, I got little sleep that night.

At 9:00 a.m., I heard the first of my morning crew coming in. Thank God, it was Eric. As soon as he entered the building, I commanded him to grab the electronic key and let me out. I told him to block the door so no other employees could enter, then I headed up to get some fresh clothes on before April arrived. I came back down and grabbed my soiled clothes off the floor with their disgusting payload and took them right out back to the commercial dumpster. I lost a good pair of jeans that day, but it was well worth it to cover up the scene of the crime. I jokingly told Eric that if he mentioned this to anyone, he would be fired on the spot. I don't think he took that as a joke, and I never heard about it from anyone. It's good to be king.

May 2010

Our lawsuit was filed and got a lot of attention, but we could not get a judge to even look at it. You see, if you've never seen the movie *Training Day*, the judges, the police, and the politicians are all on the same page. They aren't interested in our rights, only their self-interests. This movie is LA to the core.

June 9 was fast approaching, and we were trying to get a TRO (a temporary injunction) against the city until our case was decided in court, but our requests were falling on deaf ears. It seemed we were being stone-walled into closing.

Chapter 17: Battle Stations

June 2010

David Welch had exhausted every effort to get one judge to hear our case. We had another GAPP meeting, and everyone was seeking his advice on what we should do. It was June 7, and we were ordered to close June 9. Now these deadlines had come and gone before, but now the city attorney, district attorney, federal agents, and city council were all on the same page.

David Welch had it from inside sources that the raid would begin early June 10, and they would not stop until every store was closed.

"To be clear, David," I said. "They are saying that we are not allowed to use our storefronts to distribute the medicine because of the zoning ordinance, correct?"

"Correct," was David's response.

"So if we delivered the product to people's homes, that would not be violating the ordinance, correct?"

"Correct," David responded.

"OK guys, David is recommending we close our storefronts, and I, for one, do not want to be raided. I recommend you come up with a delivery model and contact your entire patient database. We need to beat these idiots at their own game. If you choose to remain open, it's at your own risk and peril."

With that the meeting ended. Most agreed we should close down for a time and let the storm blow over.

I went to Home Depot and purchased a bright orange chain and chained the front door for dramatic effect the night before the closure was to occur.

June 8, 6:00 a.m.

I was sleeping in the apartment when I heard a rap, rap, rap, on my door.

"Dalton, its Fred," he said. "You've got to wake up and see what's happening outside."

Fred was beside himself. "Oh my God, there is every news station in the book outside. ABC, NBC, Fox…they all want to talk to you."

"Oh shit, Fred, can you run down to 7-Eleven and grab me a Red Bull?" I asked. "I'll jump in the shower."

"Sure," he promised and snuck out the back door.

I peered out the window and, sure enough, there were vehicles everywhere, with telescoping antennas that went fifty feet in the air. Every major station was there. I felt like the groundhog on Groundhog's Day.

I went to the back gate to step outside and smoke a cigarette, as Fred returned with my Red Bull. I gulped it down quickly and took some heavy drags on my smoke.

Now Fred must have been noticed because soon a man and a camera crew was coming down the back alley. It was John, with *The LA Times*.

"Dalton! Dalton! Can I get an interview?" he asked.

"Sure John, but just you," I said. He brought his crew around, and we closed the gate. We entered through the back of the dispensary.

"Now, let me go talk to these guys real quick," I said. I unchained the front door and stepped outside, only to be mobbed with reporters.

"I'm sorry guys, but I'm not giving interviews. You guys never report the truth."

The Fox guy said he took great offense to that and proceeded to tell me about his aunt who was a patient.

"I will make this one statement," I said, "The politicians and police in this town are corrupt. We have every right to do what the people of the State of California decided, and we will be seeing the city attorney in court."

"Are you going to close or stay open?" they asked, as I closed the door in their faces. By now, I had had it with all the fake reporting pretending like there was some huge upsurge against these dispensaries. Nobody cares but dirty corrupt officials.

John was very thankful to get an exclusive interview. I was thankful he was falling right into my trap.

He didn't realize it at the time, and probably still doesn't realize it to this day, but I was using him as a pawn in my game and he was fulfilling his role perfectly.

You see, there were the questions everyone wanted to ask me, such as "Was I going to close?" But sometimes the answers are not what they appear. I wanted to appear to be closing for sure to get the federal agents off my back, but I had no fucking intention of halting my operations. I was just dodging their first blow, so I could land a side punch later. For all their years of studying the law, these people didn't have street smarts.

I asked John if I could have my dog, Oreo, in the photo. (People love animals, right?) I put on my saddest face. John directly asked me a question, and I directly answered it or so everyone thought.

"So you have been ordered to close your doors by Stephen Cooley, the district attorney of LA," he said. "What do you plan to do?"

"Well, John, of course you know I am a law-abiding citizen. I did not come here to break any laws, and I certainly don't want to be arrested. So, of course, I am going to follow the law."

John Hoffman, the district attorney, and the whole City of LA, as well as the rest of the country, thought I had just agreed to close down. That's what I wanted them to think, but that's not what I said...

Let's look at what I said again.

"I'm a law-abiding citizen." True.

"I don't want to be arrested." Also true.

"I am planning on following the law." Again, true. The laws of the State of California gave me every right to continue doing exactly what I was doing. I had a license on my door, and I paid excise taxes to the state. The law said I could sell marijuana, and I planned on continuing to do so.

But going along with the charade, I pretended to be sad and allowed sad photos to be taken.

Look it up. The headlines the next day said, "LA Dispensary Owners Close Their Doors With a Whimper." Mission accomplished. They had been duped.

All the stores that didn't close were raided the very next day. There were only five in the GAPP that remained open. The owners were all arrested.

"This is chess, not checkers," I thought. "Lose a battle to win the war."

We waited three days until all the raids had stopped and then began our delivery service. It was one of the first delivery services in the country. Good old American ingenuity.

July 2010

Delivery came with its own challenges and obstacles. I mean, we didn't want to walk into an undercover cop operation or have our drivers get robbed.

I decided that, for our safety, we need to have a two-tiered system. Luckily, we were starting with a huge advantage as we had a database of 3,500 patients.

If they called us and wanted a delivery, we would first send our manager, Fred. He had no money or product with him at the time. He went there to verify who this person was and that their ID matched their delivery address. If everything checked out, Fred would then call our drivers, and they would arrive with a briefcase full of smokables and edibles.

This model worked like a charm, and our business dropped by about 25 percent, but it was still enough to pay the bills. I had to lay off a few employees, which saved me a lot in labor, so profitability was about the same.

A few nights later, I saw some local cops whining on TV that many stores had not really closed but had just changed business models. You see, they said they were concerned about disrupting the neighborhoods with all the traffic, so we eliminated that worry, and they still weren't happy.

They were really just worried about greed and power. Bottom line. How could somebody getting a delivery at their house bother anyone? How was it any different than ordering a pizza?

One day, the cops tried to outsmart us. It was so obvious that it was sad and pathetic. This guy from Culver City called us and said he was staying in a hotel and needed his meds. We simply explained we did not deliver to hotels, only personal residences. We were frustrating them and thwarting their authority.

*　*　*

David Welch was able to get our case in front of a judge, and the judge agreed with us! The judge said that he was considering a TRO on the district attorney and the city attorney's office and that we were to be left alone until the court ruled on the new ordinance. The judge said this ordinance on its surface appeared to be very flawed, using zoning to shut down stores without providing the proper maps and studies.

In other words, if something is legal but requires a certain zoning (e.g., a strip club), you cannot just decide where they are *not* allowed without also mapping out where they *are* allowed.

This was great news! I called another meeting of the GAPP to discuss.

"Does this mean we can reopen?" was the question of the night?

"I cannot advise you to reopen," David said. "The ordinance is still in place. They can still raid you and arrest you."

I stayed silent. I knew what David was saying and as an attorney of course he couldn't advise that we break the law, but I was there, and I saw what the judge had said. He had said to leave us alone until he decides.

That night, I sent the letter to the GAPP. As president of the GAPP, I was personally reopening my store and advising everyone to do the same. There is strength in numbers, and we needed to hang together or we would surely hang separately.

The next day, 80 percent of the stores reopened on my advice. Two days later, David Welch was called before the judge. He called me the night before and scolded me for telling the stores to reopen. He said it put him in an awkward position with the court. I apologized but reminded him that I was the president of the organization and my job was to keep us open under the law. His job was to defend us.

It seemed that someone from the district attorney's office was on my email list. They had a copy of the email and were presenting it to the judge.

David stood in front of the judge the next day as the city attorney's offices complained that we had reopened. He even quoted a line that David Welch had given me, "We do not have to close our doors until a judge orders us to do so."

The judge agreed with me. Again, the city attorney's office was threatened with a TRO if they touched me or anyone in my organization.

We had won the day. Later, I received a text from David Welch in the evening. He told me the reopening was the right thing to do. It felt good to be right.

Chapter 18: Pulling the Tail of the Tiger

T he LAPD and the federal agents didn't like the fact they were now being somewhat restrained from raiding our stores, so they had to bring their operations underground. Rumors started flying about unreported "raids" or shakedowns that were happening across the city.

You see, normally police forces are held in check by oversight by federal agencies, such as the FBI. As we have all come to learn with the recent Comey scandal, the FBI is one of the dirtiest crime syndicates on the planet. In LA, instead of doing oversight, they have seven federal agents who are also members of the LAPD. When these drug raids occur, they can basically take whatever they want and report whatever they want. Cash, drugs, guns, cars, and even big screen TVs become part of the bounty, and these dirty cops take full advantage.

The store on Washington Street called Organica was raided. This was one of the original stores and was only a few blocks away. It was quite humorous, actually, because the federal agents, along with the LAPD coconspirators, actually broke into the ATM at this location. I guess they considered *all* money part of the bounty. But in their unadulterated greed, they failed to realize that they had just committed a felony, as the ATM was owned by a bank. The dumb motherfuckers had just robbed a bank.

Two of the members of the GAPP were raided. They were so traumatized after the raid they just dropped out of the business. The police had threatened their lives and their livelihood. If they couldn't shut us down using legal means, they would use other methods.

One of their favorite tactics was to turn us over to the IRS, another corrupt institution, as we have seen with the recent IRS scandal under Obama. You see, they used IRS codes to declare our industry and illegal operation. This means we had to pay tax on 100 percent of the earnings without writing off any expense. This meant rent, employees, and costs of good were not legitimate write-offs. Any scam the dirty crooks could use to enforce their will was fair game in their mind.

After another GAPP meeting, I learned one of our stores was dropping out of our lawsuit. I was concerned perhaps that he too had been hit by an illegal raid or worse.

The store was called the 420 Café, and it was located in Compton, one of the most Dangerous areas of LA.

I called the store and spoke with the owner, who was named Chris. Because I knew we were constantly being taped, I didn't want to discuss things on the phone, so I requested a face-to-face meeting. I also had some flower to move so was hoping he would pick some up.

The next day, I arranged to meet him at his location in Compton. Now, I will tell you, being a small town white boy, I really didn't know what I was getting into going to Compton. Compton was about an hour south of the Rainforest. When I located the storefront, I immediately began looking for parking. I wanted to be as close to the store as possible as I was carrying 2 lb. of weed and $10,000 from an earlier delivery, and the area looked worse than rough.

Fortunately, I found a metered spot about a half a block away in view of the storefront. I exited the car and secured my backpack as I put coins in the meter. As I began walking toward the store, I could hear some loud "ghetto" music booming in front of the store. As I got closer, I could see a black Cadillac parked directly in front of the store with about six young

Black men surrounding the vehicle. They all definitely took notice as I approached.

Now I can't say I wasn't a little nervous walking through this group of obvious gang bangers, but I also realized they were the security for the store. They must be on Chris's payroll. Who wants to fuck with a gang? Unless it's another gang, of course. As I reached for the door, one of the men came over and said, "Let me get that for you" as he entered with me. He quickly struck up a conversation to find out who I was and who I was here to see.

"I'm a friend of Chris," I said, not really knowing if I would even recognize Chris if I saw him. We had over a hundred members in our organization.

"Oh, cool man, I'm a friend of Chris also," the man said with a smile and gave me the LA handshake. "Let me know if there's anything I can do for you," he said as he walked back to the street entrance.

I walked up to the receptionist, and she invited me to have a seat.

"You're Dalton from the Rainforest, aren't you?" She asked, like she was meeting a celebrity. "I've heard about you and how you are winning the fight against the city," she said in complete admiration.

"I sure hope we are winning," I said.

"Oh my God! We just got our license today," she exclaimed and pointed to a document on the wall.

I tried not to stare, but I could tell this was a legitimate document on city letterhead. It was signed by a city clerk and the city attorney. It was a license to legally operate a dispensary in LA.

The truly, truly amazing part about this was that no such document existed. We were months, if not years, away from getting to the actual licensing of dispensaries in LA. I did not say anything to the young lady. I was just in shock.

"What the hell is going on?" I asked myself.

About five minutes went by, and then the receptionist said, "Come with me; Chris is ready for you."

We got to the back office and she opened the door. Nope, I surely didn't recognize Chris. He must have joined the GAPP at a later time after our initial meetings.

Chris was not a man you could ever forget meeting. He had to be close to 400 lb. and Samoan. He did not bother standing up but reached across the desk to shake my hand. By his smile, I could tell he knew who I was and he asked me to have a seat. First, we made small talk, but I was dying to jump into the conversation, so I did at the first opportunity.

"So Chris, I hear you are dropping out of the lawsuit," I said, a little dumbfounded. "Why would you do that? We are winning."

"I know, Dalton, but I don't need it anymore," he said, kind of sheepishly. "You see, I'm not really the owner anymore."

"Oh, I see," I said. "Yeah, your receptionist was super excited that you got your new license. Chris, that's amazing because both you and I know that there is no such thing..." I looked at him with a half-smile. "Huh?"

"Oh, come on, Dalton. You're in LA. Everything is available for a price," he said as if I didn't know that.

"I see, Chris. Well, Chris, you know who I am. You know I've stuck my neck out for each and every one of you, risking my freedom and my life for all of our rights, right?"

"Yeah, Dalton. You've been amazing. Thank you. You are a decent guy, and everyone knows that."

"OK, so If I wanted to get a 'license,' how much would it cost me, and who would I have to pay?" I inquired. "Could you help make that happen?"

"The price is $250,000, and all I can say is I'll talk to some people," he promised.

"OK, Chris. I'll be honest. I'm tired. If these people wanted to buy me out, I would walk away."

"OK, I'll let them know," he promised again.

"Now on to other things. Do you guys need any flower?" I asked him as I pulled out my merchandise. I was carrying OG and LA Confidential. He looked at it but said they were super stocked right now, so no thanks.

With that, we shook hands, and I walked toward the door. "Here's my cell phone," I said, "but be careful as I'm being taped by federal agents all the time."

"Got it," Chris said.

As I exited the shop, my new gang banger friend escorted me to my car.

"Catch you later, man," he said as I entered my vehicle.

Wow, I felt like a "connected man" with that type of treatment.

My mind was racing on the drive back to my store. "LA is living up to its reputation as the most corrupt city in the US, I guess," I thought. My image of the US as the bastion of freedom and democracy was dying fast. This was like living in a third-world nation.

With the recent activity of raids, my manager Fred and I decided we should move the bulk of our inventory off site just in case. After all, we had over 30 lb. of weed on location, half of which was on consignment from vendors and other stores, so if we were raided not only would we lose everything, but we would have half of LA after us for repayment.

But where could we store 30 lb. of pot safely? You see, when these Gestapo police come in to raid you, they leave no stone unturned, so if you were paying rent on another location, they would just connect the dots and track down that location too. They could seize your bank records and trace it to your hidden stash. I was faced with a dilemma. How could I set up such a place in someone else's name?

Luckily, my thirty-year-old son was visiting town, so we set up two different storage facilities nearby. Everything was put in his name, so nothing could be tracked to me. I was just listed as someone who had access, as well as Fred. When we decided to move the bulk of our stuff, we took three separate vans, two of which were dummy vans containing nothing and the third contained the goods. We loaded fake duffle bags into the two dummies, then the third with the real stuff.

It might sound silly, but we knew we were being watched so we had to take extra precautions.

I slept much easier once we had all of our product secured.

I called Mike, the private investigator, and, like an idiot, I told him what I had discovered at the 420 Café.

He said he would look into it. I never heard from this man again and when I called, his number had been disconnected.

After a week, I grew impatient, so I decided to go pay my friend Chris a surprise visit to see if I could get any updates. I also wanted to get an actual photo of the "fake license" in case I ever needed it.

When I arrived at the location, I was shocked. There were boards all over the front of the store. I found parking and started walking toward the store to find out what had happened. I was hoping I would locate my gang banger friend but I had no such luck.

There was, however, a young Black man leaning against the wall. He appeared to be on some type of drug, but he made eye contact with me as I approached, so I thought it was worth a shot.

"Hey man, what happened to this store?" I asked, perplexed.

"The cops shut it down," the man said as he leaned his head back and peered into my eyes.

What? I was confused. Why would cops shut down a store that was being "protected" by some higher up in the city?

"You mean they got raided?" I asked in disbelief. Why would police raid a connected store?

"No, man. No, the cops pulled up to the back and just loaded everything up. They moved, I guess," he said.

"Ohhh," I said. I was dumbfounded.

As I got in the car and started heading back to Mar Vista, something hit me. "They were scared of me."

I had just enough fame, power, knowledge, and contacts to bring them down. That's why they closed down the store. I was on to them, and they knew it. Remember my telephone threats to my illegal listeners?

"If anything happens to me, all this information is being held at seven attorneys and will go directly to the *Wall Street Journal*." I had them in a stalemate. For now, anyway. I wonder what they did or said to my private investigator to get him to disappear. I'll probably never know.

I think Americans, for the most part, still live in this fantasy world that we live in "the land of the free." That's true as long as you do everything the government tells you to do. Try skipping out on your taxes and bills and see how "free" you are. They will take everything you own, toss you out on the street, and then arrest you for vagrancy. A man in Arizona lost his whole family in an accident, which threw him into a real depression. Soon he lost his job and his house. He was so distraught by the loss of his family that he packed up a survival pack and just went to live in the Arizona wilderness. He lived in a cave for two years but then was found out by the federal authorities. He was arrested for trespassing on federal land.

Trespassing? How can you trespass on your own land? Isn't this a government of the people, by the people, and for the people? That is the people's land. The federal government doesn't own shit. They are the stewards of our land. That's it. The grounds keepers. They are the servants and not the master…or that's how it's supposed to be, anyway.

In reality, the deep state has taken over our country. We have presidents elected for four- or eight-year terms, and we have representatives in Congress with no term limits. As these legislatures become more and more controlled by big money, the deep state federal police agencies keep their eyes and ears open.

Did you know that the number one users of overseas bank accounts are dirty politicians and so-called nonprofits? Remember a few years ago, back in the Obama administration, when the US for the first time in history was able to crack open the Swiss bank accounts? Even the Nazis were not able to do this.

Do you remember the aftermath with all the arrests of corrupt public figures? Do you remember? Neither do I because nobody was arrested. Why? Because that's not what federal police do. That's not how they operate. They are not interested in arresting you. They are interested in money and power.

If they catch a politician having sex with a minor or selling influence to foreign powers, they simply approach that politician and give him an offer he can't refuse. Either we can arrest you, destroy your career, and embarrass your family or you can "play ball." You do what we tell you to do from now on. You get to keep your power and your good name. We just share in the profits. The deep state owns half the politicians in DC.

With these new revelations that the cops knew I was investigating them, I decided a little vacation in Mexico was warranted. Now that I knew the true depth of their corruption, I also decided I need to start stashing cash outside the store. But where could I put it?

In another power move by the police to try to shut us down, the Gestapo had started warning all banks that if we deposited funds or took credit cards, the bank was participating in a felony. They were forcing us underground. We could only take cash and had nowhere to deposit.

One of my bank accounts was frozen by Chase bank with $40,000 in it. They said I could have it back in two years. I decided the only safe place to store it was at my girlfriend's house in Mexico.

Now I know what you are thinking. You're going to store tens of thousands of dollars with a stripper in Mexico? Sounds crazy, huh? But not as crazy as trusting our government to follow the law and to obey our rights. That's really crazy. Over the next few weeks, I took over fifty thousand and stored it in the walls of my girlfriend's house. Angela was in love with me—real love. I wasn't worried. We had also discovered that she was pregnant so we began planning our wedding. I planned to bring her on a fiancée visa in the future once things settled down.

Now I must emphasize at this point that this was during the height of the Mexican drug cartel wars in northern Mexico. The Adelita Bar, where Angela worked, was owned by the Tijuana cartel, which was run by a pair of brothers. The Hong Kong hotel was owned by the Sinaloa cartel from central Mexico. These two cartels were at war, but they never let it come into the hotel district. That would be bad for business.

One day, I was driving to Angela's apartment, and there was a body hanging from the bridge. I guess an honest police chief had tried to interfere in cartel operations. They killed his whole family.

During this time period, the Tijuana cartel was wiped out by the Sinaloa cartel, with the backing of the US government. Remember the Fast and the Furious scandal under Obama? We got caught selling guns to the Sinaloa cartel on a "sting" operation? Obama's attorney general, Eric Holder, was the first attorney general in US history to be held in contempt of congress for not cooperating. Obama used executive privilege to skirt the facts. Americans are so gullible. And still I felt safer in Tijuana than I did in my own country. That should tell you something.

Chapter 19: Rise of Kamala Harris
September to October 2010

One day, while sitting in the office of the dispensaries, one of my employees, Marco, walked in all distraught.

"What's going on, Marco?" I asked.

"The cops just stole my car," he said, almost ready to cry.

"Stole your car? The cops?"

"What, did you get busted with weed in the car?" I asked.

"No, I was just driving to work and they had a check point in the Albertson's parking lot. They made me pull over and checked my registration, driver's license, and insurance. Because all the addresses and information didn't match, they confiscated the car for a minimum of thirty days. A minimum of thirty days," he repeated.

"After thirty days, if I have all my paperwork updated, they will give it back, but I must pay towing fees and impound fees of $85 per day for thirty days. Dalton, the car is only worth about three grand. I can't afford that. They just stole my car," he said again.

I was visibly disgusted with the Nazi tactics. If you live in small town America, you really have no idea how far gone these police forces are. They are so desperate for power and money that they don't care about your rights.

Why do you think groups like BLM have formed? I promise you it's not because of a few bad cops. Not all cops are bad, but I assure you all cops know cops who are bad. Therefore, since they are cops, it's their duty to arrest the bad cops or they are guilty by association. They are not keeping their oath to protect and serve. The following week, shortly after I left for Mexico, ten uniformed police officers showed up at my dispensary. At first, my employees thought we were being raided, but these were local LAPD, not federal agents.

They stated they had a gun report called in to them, so they needed to search the entire premises.

Right away, Fred got me on the phone, just as I arrived in San Ysidro on the frontier with Mexico.

The police officer on the line promised he was not interested in our marijuana only for guns.

Now, by law, a dispensary owner was not allowed to have a gun on the premises as they considered that a felony since I was "illegally" dealing a narcotic. If they found a gun on the premises, I would be arrested for sure. I was safe because I had taken my Ruger with me in the car. Lucky for me, I was not in the shop. Still another example of how our rights have been taken away. What right in hell does any government body have to tell me I can't carry a gun? Answer: None. See second amendment for clarification.

November was coming fast and the GAPP had decided we need to get involved in the upcoming elections. We had two people in our cross hairs. First was Stephen Cooley, my arch nemesis by this time, who was running for attorney general of the state of California. If he won, he vowed to close down all dispensaries across the state. He was running on the Republican ticket against the district attorney of San Francisco. Yes, Kamala Harris. When we first realized we had an opportunity to defeat him, we contacted all two hundred of the GAPP dispensaries and got people registered to vote. We started our "Cooley is not cool" campaign.

Once we decided on this course of action, I decided to reconnect with the publisher of *Weed World Magazine*, Mike. Now mind you, he had over a hundred GAPP advertisers, and I was sure he would join our cause. I set up an appointment to meet him in the offices of his publication.

As I sat down, I very enthusiastically started telling him about our plans to defeat Cooley. He listened until I was finished, then he rained on my parade.

"Dalton, I admire what you are trying to do, but Cooley is too well financed and too popular. I'm sorry, Dalton, but there is no way you can win. We can't afford to draw the attention of law enforcement, which is already targeting our type of magazine."

I blew my top. "Are you kidding me, Mike? We risk our asses every day, and you profit heavily. Now when we need you to join the fight, you're going to sit this one out?"

"I'm sorry, Dalton. I have investors to worry about."

"Well, sometimes you have to worry about principles, Mike. Tell your investors this. They either join us in this fight, or we will blacklist you from any more advertising."

"I'm sorry you feel that way, Dalton, but we can't. I'm sorry."

"That's fine, Mike. The GAPP is done with you. Goodbye," And that was it. We pulled all of our ads. But that's not the best part. Election day came. It was a close race. By midnight, Cooley declared victory. I smoked a bowl with Susan. By 1:00 a.m., the ticker kept moving in Kamala's favor. By morning, Kamala Harris had pulled ahead by .25 percent in LA county. In the end, we had registered well over 100,000 voters to vote against Cooley.

Kamala won by 75,000 votes. People that knew gave me full credit for the upset. The GAPP defeated Cooley. We were now even more famous.

The other contest we were involved in was Jose Huizar of Eagle Rock. This guy was born in the Zacatecas region of Mexico. I bet you will never guess what their favorite crop in Zacatecas, Mexico, is? You guessed it. Zacatecas purple, a very popular strain. Any guesses how a farmer in Zacatecas, Mexico, could send his son to Princeton University in the US and to become a city councilman in LA?

So Huizar was being challenged by a very popular restaurant operator and reality show star. Guizar was not well liked, and everyone knew he was dirty to the core. Election night, the votes were neck and neck, then of course the next day Huizar had 5,000 in absentee ballots arrive. The election was stolen. Typical California corruption at its best. It brings me great joy to see he was arrested this last year as a sitting councilman for racke-teering. Good riddance to bad rubbish. He must have fallen out of favor with the cartels and the dirty cops. They all eventually turn on each other.

Chapter 20: Escape from LA

In late October, I got back on a Monday to the shop after spending another weekend with Angela. Our baby was due in early November. We were making her home ready for the new arrival. I was forty-five years old and getting ready to be a new papa. My two sons I had from a previous marriage were now in their mid-twenties, but I was happy and in love. We had completed the fiancée visa process, so now Angela was able to come across the border. We planned on having the baby in a hospital in Chula Vista, California, a place with no ties to the business. In case there was a raid and arrest, I didn't want her visa to be revoked. Again, these corrupt officials couldn't care less about breaking up families as long as they can line their own pockets. Without a family, I was untouchable.

Now I had a weak spot. I didn't know which side of the border was safe, as the federal agents were in bed with the cartels. For the first time, since this whole ordeal began, I felt vulnerable.

My baby was born November 6, 2009. Five fingers, five toes. I decided I wanted to keep it that way, so I started planning my escape from LA. I had had my fun poking the tiger but now with a new family I needed to protect them. Angela and I flew to Las Vegas to get married. We stayed at the Stratosphere and got married at the Little White Chapel. If you can imagine a little girl from Tabasco, Mexico, it was all spectacular and overwhelming. We took a limo out to the Hoover Dam. The baby slept the whole way. I knew I was doing the right thing by protecting my family.

I got further confirmation when two of my grow facilities were raided, one in Oakland, California and the other in LA County. Both were raided within two weeks of their harvest time. You see the dirty cops were just letting us do all the work so they could cultivate our crops and resell them on the open market. One of my growers, who had financed the La Grow facility, lost his entire investment. Jesse was a decent family man and when the raid came, they went to his house and busted in his door with his four children home. They pinned him and his wife to the floor as they dissected his house, bit by bit. The police took his hunting rifles, his televisions, and all the money in his safe. At the grow facility, they "harvested" all the plants and smashed all of his grow lights. Each one cost over a thousand dollars. They did not arrest Jesse but said they were considering pressing charges. You see, the police tactic was to steal everything you own and then threaten to press charges until you just go away. My attorney, David Welch, told me I was on the FBI's person of interest list and that it might be a good idea to get out of California. I decided he was right and thought I could run the store remotely from Arizona.

I had been speaking to Mark about an opportunity in Arizona to open up a school. It seemed Arizona and Colorado were both considering medical and recreational marijuana. Greenway University was the first licensed school in the nation to teach the growing and processing of marijuana.

I flew up to Colorado to partake in some educational seminars that this university was putting on, and the opportunity looked legitimate. At the first seminar, they asked me if I would be a greeter, to kind of get a feel for the whole operation, and I agreed to do so.

People started to file into the conference room at about 2:00 p.m., and there was a "buzz" of excitement, pardon the pun. You could tell people were incredibly happy to be around like-minded people, and it was a festive atmosphere. As I stood in the doorway, an older Hispanic man entered the room. As I walked over to greet him, I saw a very distinct DEA emblem on his polo shirt.

"I'm sorry, sir, but we do not allow DEA agents into our marijuana conference," I said jokingly.

"Well, I'm retired," he said with a gleeful playfulness in his eyes.

"Well OK, then that's a different story," I said, keeping the banter going. "Now let me ask you, what are you hoping to get out of today's session?" I inquired intensely.

"Well, I'm just checking this out for my son," he said. "My son wants to be a grower."

"I see, well then you came to the right place, sir. Come with me." I began to escort him to his seat.

At that point, he pulled me aside and said, "You know, it's an interesting story, but when I did work for the DEA, back in the 1980s, I was a pilot. It was my job to fly planeloads of cocaine from Columbia or Costa Rica into the US. You see, we were setting up a 'sting' operation and trying to look like a big player. What was really interesting is that each of us had to sign a classified document stating that if we ever got caught, we could not acknowledge to anyone that this was a government operation. In other words, we had to 'take the fall.' They assured us they would get us out of prison later once everything blew over."

"That is interesting, indeed," I said as we reached his chair. "Enjoy the conference."

As I headed back to the front door, the full weight of what this man had just said hit me.

You see, if you know anything about the 1980s, the streets were so packed with cocaine, they couldn't possibly sell anymore. This is when Ronald Reagan announced his War on Drugs and the "Just Say No" campaign. In fact, there was so much cocaine on the street that the government actually had to invent a more addictive use of cocaine to increase usage because the reality of the situation was that US government has always been in the cocaine business. This is how and why crack cocaine was invented and distributed to the inner city Black communities. These communities were decimated. Men were imprisoned and families shattered, just so crooked politicians could make a buck. Is it any wonder we have Black Lives Matter protestors burning down our cities today?

The most interesting thing this man had told me he didn't even realize. He was not part of a sting operation, although he earnestly believed he was. He was simply a mule for the DEA—a drug runner.

I wonder if this will ever dawn on him. I wonder how many cops think they are doing the right thing by doing the wrong thing?

I met with the owner of Greenway, Gustavo Escobar, after the session, and he and Mark convinced me Arizona was ripe for the picking. He told me for $75,000 I could have the whole Arizona territory.

I was excited to get back to Arizona and away from the corruption of LA. A week before Christmas, I packed up my family from Chula Vista, packed my $50,000 stash in my leather jacket pocket, and set out on Interstate 8.

Now for those of you who don't know, all along the southern border with Mexico, our highways contain "checkpoints." These checkpoints are supposedly to look for two things: illegals and drugs.

Ninety percent of the time, these checkpoints will have K-9 dogs to sniff each car as it passes. It worried me a little to have to go through these points because if you think about it, I lived in a marijuana dispensary, so my clothes all reeked of marijuana. I thought it might be a much better choice to shoot north through the Temecula area, then go up to Interstate 10, which had no checkpoints. My fear, knowing my luck, was perhaps I had forgotten a joint in my car somewhere and the dog would find it. Then I'd be screwed and they could deport my wife and child.

But I was 99 percent confident there was nothing in the car but my smelly clothes, and going north would add three hours to a five-hour drive. So, I opted to take the Interstate 8. What I failed to realize, and it still haunts me to this day, is that if they find money in large amounts and have suspicion of drugs or marijuana, they can confiscate the money. Had I known that, I would have never attempted to drive down Interstate 8.

So here I was approaching the first checkpoint, nervous as hell. Now let me say this, it is sad that a grown man has to worry about losing everything he owns because of a plant. It is sad we have illegal search and seizures occurring in violation of the fourth amendment. These violations of our basic rights are what has led to the rise of Trump.

At the first checkpoint, I was very lucky. The K-9 unit flagged another car just in front of me, so they exited to the side and I glided right though. So far, so good.

The second checkpoint we came into right after Yuma, Arizona. As we approached, the dog circled each car intently, then it was our turn. As soon as the dog got close, it started spinning and jumping and barking at my vehicle. It had a hit! And that was me. My heart was racing.

The officer walked over to the window, and I rolled it down. He continued to inform me that the dog had identified my vehicle as having either narcotics or a hidden person in the vehicle. He said, "Don't worry, though, because sometimes babies give a false positive."

He asked me to pull over, so I did.

He asked us to step out of the vehicle and told us we could go into the waiting area. I told him I preferred to watch the search. At that point, I pulled out my medical marijuana card and informed the officer who I was and what I did for a living. He was unimpressed. I told him it was probably my clothes giving off the aroma as I sold marijuana in two stores in LA and San Diego. He informed me if they even found a seed, I would be "processed." After all I had endured, this comment just struck a nerve.

There were two officers, both in their early twenties, I would guess, and I decided to educate them on the real world while they searched for evidence to ruin my life.

"I'm sure you guys think you're doing pretty important work here, don't you?" I asked.

"Just protecting our country first," one said. Now this guy had all the attitude you would expect from an arrogant wannabe cop. He handled the dog, and the dog repeatedly entered my vehicle, dragging in dog hair as he searched. He kept pointing at the suitcases so the other officer removed them and put them on a table for closer examination. The second officer seemed younger and nicer. He had red hair, blue eyes, and a polite mannerism.

"Protecting our country, are you? From what? Old men who smoke a joint every once in a while?" I responded sarcastically.

This only fueled the young robo-cop on. He was determined to get me now.

"If you want to really arrest some bad guys, I'd recommend arresting your bosses. They are the biggest drug dealers in this country, young man. The war on drugs is a war against the American people, young man. And let me tell you something. If you declare war on the American people, you will always lose."

The red-haired man's search of my bags came up empty. My leather jacket with the $50,000 in it laid on the passenger seat. The dog never looked at it. Neither did the officers.

Finally the GI Joe realized he wasn't going to find anything and said," Yeah, it must have been the clothes."

"I tried to tell you, young man. But you were just doing your job. Think about what I said to you. I promise you, you are on the wrong side of the law."

With that, we were on our way. No more checkpoints.

A week later, I was reading an article that a stripper had been pulled over in LA when moving to Florida, and they discovered a million dollars in her trunk. It was confiscated for two years until she could prove she earned it honestly. Guilty until proven innocent, I guess. I would have been so screwed if they had taken my cash. It would have been life altering.

As I arrived in Arizona, I already had a house waiting for me. Remember the gay couple who had rented my house? Well, it seemed they had a falling out, and one had killed the other. Not in my house, thank God. But now the other was in jail. Strange how life happens.

After being in Arizona for only a week, I got news that my dispensary had gotten served several lawsuits, one from the city of LA. I guess they had not been embarrassed enough from our last encounter. Also Jose Huizar's office was pursuing litigation for some voting registration error I supposedly committed. I guess he didn't like the fact that we were trying to oust him.

On top of that, it seemed my old friend Brian Kim was now suing me for kicking him out of the store. I also found out that Greenway University was a total scam, and both Mark and Gustavo were convicted felons. With this new information, I demanded they give me my $75,000 back, which resulted in another lawsuit. I sent out an email to the GAPP informing everyone that Gus and Mark were con artists and got hit by another lawsuit for defamation. When it rains, it pours. It amazed me that in my forty-five years, I had never before even been in a lawsuit, and now I was a party to five.

Never before had I been in trouble with the law, but now I was a person of interest with the FBI. In fact, my first week in Arizona, I was driving down the road, contemplating all this legal action, when all of a sudden, I decided to pull into a Circle K from the middle lane. I checked my rearview mirror, and there were no cars in my blind spot, so I zipped over with screeching tires.

To my surprise, another car did the same.

"How odd," I thought. I walked over to a pay phone and pretended to make a phone call as I turned toward the car. Just like you see in the movies, the car was black with tinted windows. I lit up a cigarette as I watched the car pull up to a gas pump. I stood there staring at the car until finally a gentleman stepped out. It was a man dressed in a suit with silver/gray hair. He pretended not to look my way, but I could see he was eyeing me from the side. Once he walked into the building, I immediately walked over to his car and circled it. There was not even a plate on the car. I knew right then I was being followed.

Facing five lawsuits and being investigated, for what I don't know, I had two choices: fight or flee.

As a student of history, I knew all too well that it is nearly impossible to win a war, fighting on two fronts. Here, I was faced with the possibility of a five-front war. Enemies were surrounding me, and I had a family to protect. If fighting was no longer an option and fleeing was not possible, that only left me with one more escape.

I created a third option: to hide in plain sight. I perfected a method called ghosting, a method to carry on day-to-day activities, buy and sell houses, make great money, and always remain under the radar. For the next ten years, my family and I disappeared off the grid. This is my first reappearance. My son is ten now. We have a good life under a different name. In ten years, many things have changed. What I was doing back then is nothing compared to what is going on today. Now nobody cares what I did back then. Back then, it was cutting edge. Now over thirty states have made marijuana legal. This is a direct result of the fights and sacrifices of many brave patriots who were willing to sacrifice everything for our freedoms.

Since our government can't make money selling marijuana anymore, they just tax the crap out of it. Now their cash crop is opioids. This is why the war in Afghanistan has been going on for twenty years. It's all about the poppy seed. My question to all Americans is: When are you going to wake up? When are we going to take out country back?

That is a task for younger men, I'm afraid. Our government has been at war with our people for decades. The baby boomers and baby busters have let it happen.

What are you going to do? What are you willing to sacrifice? What is freedom really worth to you?

About the Author

Dalton Daniels is a serial entrepreneur, father, and husband from a small town in southwest Michigan. An entrepreneur at heart, he succeeded in his first business, an adventure club for singles in Phoenix, Arizona, where he lives with his Spanish speaking wife and their two young sons. To Dalton life is a learning adventure and he always wants to see what lies around the next corner. Definitely the road less traveled.